BENEFICIARY GUIDE
for Everyone

How to Receive What's Yours from
Estates, Trusts, and More

RONALD FARRINGTON SHARP

ALLWORTH PRESS
NEW YORK

Copyright © 2025 by Ronald Farrington Sharp

All rights reserved. Copyright under Berne Copyright Convention, Universal Copyright Convention, and Pan American Copyright Convention. No part of this book may be reproduced, stored in a retrieval system, or transmitted in any form, or by any means, electronic, mechanical, photocopying, recording or otherwise, without the express written consent of the publisher, except in the case of brief excerpts in critical reviews or articles. All inquiries should be addressed to Allworth Press, 307 West 36th Street, 11th Floor, New York, NY 10018.

Allworth Press books may be purchased in bulk at special discounts for sales promotion, corporate gifts, fundraising, or educational purposes. Special editions can also be created to specifications. For details, contact the Special Sales Department, Allworth Press, 307 West 36th Street, 11th Floor, New York, NY 10018 or info@skyhorsepublishing.com.

29 28 27 26 25   5 4 3 2 1

Published by Allworth Press, an imprint of Skyhorse Publishing, Inc. 307 West 36th Street, 11th Floor, New York, NY 10018. Allworth Press® is a registered trademark of Skyhorse Publishing, Inc.®, a Delaware corporation.

www.allworth.com

Cover design by Mary Belibasakis

Library of Congress Cataloging-in-Publication Data is available on file.

Print ISBN: 978-1-62153-807-3
eBook ISBN: 978-1-62153-808-0

Printed in the United States of America

> Be advised that the information in this book is not legal advice and you should always seek legal advice from an attorney, financial planner, or accountant experienced in estates, trusts, and wills. State and federal laws change frequently, so do not rely on this book for legal or tax advice.

Contents

Introduction		v
Chapter 1:	Stages of Planning	1
Chapter 2:	Revocable and Irrevocable Beneficiaries	7
Chapter 3:	If You Are the Grantor	13
Chapter 4:	Powers of Attorney	19
Chapter 5:	Trustees and Trust Directors	25
Chapter 6:	Fairness in Naming Heirs	29
Chapter 7:	The Family Cottage: Solutions to Joint Ownership Problems	35
Chapter 8:	Trusting Your Trustee	37
Chapter 9:	Ignoring the Wishes of the Deceased	43
Chapter 10:	The Family Business	47
Chapter 11:	Special Needs Trusts	53
Chapter 12:	Ladybird Deeds	59
Chapter 13:	Gifting	63
Chapter 14:	Estate Planning Using Beneficiary Designations	67
Chapter 15:	Should You Write Your Own Will or Trust?	69
Chapter 16:	How to Guarantee that Your Estate Is Probated	77
Chapter 17:	Will Contests	81
Chapter 18:	Legal Rights of Beneficiaries: Knowledge Is Power	93
Chapter 19:	Estate Planning from the Heart: Distributing a Legacy in a Heartfelt Way	99
Chapter 20:	Equal Division May Not Be Fair	105
Chapter 21:	Beneficiary Designations for Trusts and Wills	113
Chapter 22:	The Stuff, and How to Get Rid of It	127
Chapter 23:	Do You Really Want to Be the Trustee?	133

Chapter 24:	Burials and Funerals: What Is the Process?	137
Chapter 25:	Now You Are a Beneficiary	141
Chapter 26:	The Reading of the Will Ceremony	143
Chapter 27:	Unfair, Weird, Unlawful, or Impossible Will Instructions	147
Chapter 28:	Pet Trusts	151
Chapter 29:	Preserving and Accessing Digital Assets	155
Chapter 30:	Settling the Estate	159

Appendix	171
Glossary	173
Index	177

Introduction

There are two stages of successful estate planning that ensure your assets will be passed on according to your wishes. Your heirs should enjoy a smooth transfer of their inheritance based on your instructions as to who gets what from your estate, when they get it, and who is in charge of the process that will transfer your assets to your heirs according to your written instructions with no unneeded expense or delay.

The first step is to create a plan for your beneficiaries while you are still alive and competent. This step is critical and may entail a combination of revocable and irrevocable trusts, gifts, joint ownership, and beneficiary designations. Beneficiaries should be named for all intangible assets and titled assets, and specific instructions should be in place as to the designation of heirs to specific tangible assets. The goal of planning is, at the end of the day, to have no assets in your individual name or assets with no beneficiary named. We want to settle estates privately, quickly, and inexpensively. Beneficiary designations are flexible and choosing the right combination for your plan can be critical. Avoiding probate is a valuable gift to your beneficiaries.

The second step is directed to potential heirs so that they can claim transfer of assets rightfully theirs under the rules of law for intestate estates. If no plans were made ahead of death, the potential heirs should know their rights and be aware of the legal process and how it affects them. Resolving disagreements or misunderstandings with other potential heirs saves time, avoids hurt feelings, and makes a seamless transition of assets possible.

Much has been written about the pros and cons of wills and trusts. Avoiding probate is the purported advantage of trusts over wills since wills are probated and trusts are not. But a trust is not always right for everyone. There are other probate-avoiding methods for simple estates that are now being used. Planned use of beneficiary designations and pay-on-death transfer of certain assets (including real estate) should be considered as a good alternative or addition to traditional estate planning.

Everyone's goal in settling a decedent's estate should be to allow the process to be done with minimal drama, few misunderstandings, and no family estrangement. Planning is a two-part process to get the maximum benefit from beneficiary designations before death and after death.

CHAPTER 1

Stages of Planning

The first part of the estate planning process is deciding upon the appropriate type of legal plan that best suits the family situation and dispositive objectives of the person making the plan. We plan for death, but also need to plan for disability. We break this down into pre-death planning and post-death planning and procedures.

WHAT IS AN ESTATE?

A person's estate consists of everything owned at the time of death as well as what other assets come into being and rights that could accrue after death. It could also mean things that could be part of a person's assets while alive but could expire at the time of death if not used up before then. Let's break that down.

1. Everything owned at the time of death includes such things as real estate, personal property (which means tangible things like furniture, vehicles, and sports equipment), and intangible things like money, bank accounts, stocks, investments, or royalties.

2. Life insurance proceeds are paid out at the time of death. Other types of insurance or investments can also have a beneficiary and the beneficiary can be the estate (in which case they would be probated) or the trust, if any, could be the beneficiary. If a named beneficiary is a

person (or people) the proceeds are not probatable nor are they considered trust assets.

3. Some things, like some annuity contracts, are assets while a person is alive but often cease to be at time of death. Assets which a person has control over when alive and which the person can transfer ownership of, called powers of appointment, may have considerable value while a person is alive and maybe none at death. An example might be when, in a will, a donor dies and leaves an asset to someone else who is instructed to transfer that property to another person or institution of his or her choice. This is sometimes used in charitable bequests.

The goal of estate planning is to create a plan for distribution that includes who should get the assets, under what conditions, naming who will be in charge of that process, and setting up the most advantageous plan cost and time wise. This might include tax planning, probate avoidance, asset management for heirs, and planning for special needs heirs, such as the disabled or minors.

Some states have laws that approve a state promulgated fill-in-the-blank will that anyone can use to make their own will. That will would meet all the state's requirements for a legal will including specific instructions on witnessing and signing. Using this will can save the cost of an attorney-prepared simple will, but be warned: It still has to go through the probate process. Avoiding probate is one of the goals of good estate planning.

Your plan should answer all the "what ifs" that could occur and have a solution that covers those. For example, what if a named heir dies before you? Would that deceased heir's share of the estate go to that person's children or spouse, or to charity? What if the deceased heir's children are minors? Who would then be in charge of the minors' share, and under what circumstances or at what age should the minor children have their inheritance turned over to them? We want to do our best to identify situations that could, if not planned for, cause family conflict or even estrangement.

In a joint marital situation where one spouse survives the other, should provisions be made in case the survivor remarries? Would there be restrictions on the ability of a surviving spouse to amend a trust to include protections for a new partner? Should this be an irrevocable trust in which the new spouse would have the right to the use of the former marital home and an income from the former joint assets, or should the new spouse have unlimited access to the former joint assets?

Then there are the tangible assets that need to be designated to specific individuals. Who gets mom's wedding ring or other one-of-a-kind items at her death? Is there a family farm or business that needs to be kept operating, and if so, by whom? There are a lot of plans that need to be made and each family's situation is unique to them. Making no plan at all is a plan in itself. Leaving a mess behind for the heirs to sort is in fact a plan but is not a good one.

We need to lay out in clear and concise language the legal process of creating an estate plan and to anticipate some common issues that occur if the planning goes awry. I will briefly go over standard planning techniques involving wills, testamentary and living trusts, probate-avoiding techniques which do not involve trusts, and post-death procedures and issues. These subjects are covered in more detail in my series of "for everyone" books: *Living Trusts for Everyone*, *How to Avoid Probate for Everyone*, and *Settling Estates for Everyone*. I will use a broad brush in covering these topics herein and move on to common sense, but not illegal, advice on real-life situations often unanticipated by the ones making the estate plan.

There are specific ways to help heirs and families work together in dealing with the practical things that need to be done at the death of a loved one. These are not just legal actions. While dealing with grief is not the focus here, the pre- and post-death periods are typically emotional and stressful. People react sometimes in unpredictable and illogical ways to the death of a loved one and may say or do things that would otherwise seem out of character. Families are sometimes estranged over money issues and assumptions as to property disposition.

Disagreements with the deceased's instructions, the role and rights of in-laws, stepchildren, and second or third marriages are all issues that can tear families apart. Family businesses are always a difficult thing to figure out. So, seeing how others have handled situations that might exist or could arise in your own case could be helpful and can in some cases lead to actions which can ease some of the stress-fueled reactions.

If you are in the planning stage for your own estate or are assisting someone else, the scenarios presented could help you set up a plan that will lead to fewer problems than might otherwise arise. If you are an heir, executor, or trustee, you might be helped by knowing how to administer an estate efficiently while keeping in mind the expectations and fears of the heirs and beneficiaries.

Read and learn about wills and trusts: Familiarize yourself with the basics of estate planning, wills, and trusts. Understand the key concepts affecting beneficiaries, executors, trustees, and the distribution of assets. Seek professional advice from an estate planning attorney or financial planner to ensure you make informed decisions.

Create a comprehensive estate plan: Draft a will or trust that clearly outlines your wishes regarding asset distribution, guardianship of minor children (if applicable), and any specific bequests. Consider establishing a trust, which can provide additional control and flexibility in managing and distributing assets for beneficiaries over time rather than a lump-sum payout. Work with a qualified professional to create a plan tailored to your specific circumstances.

If the planning process is completed properly while the decedent is alive and competent, the beneficiaries will have the assets transferred to them quickly and without court involvement. The various legal processes for pre-death planning are explained herein with emphasis on revocable trusts and various types of beneficiary plan distributions. Powers of attorney can also be used to set up proper plans while the settlor is alive.

First, we need to narrow the focus to the kinds of beneficiaries that are out there, since beneficiaries are not just people but can be groups of people, companies, organizations, and the public at large. When we say beneficiary, what comes to mind is life insurance, but the word beneficiary encompasses more than just that.

What or who can be a beneficiary? It doesn't have to be a person, but usually is. And it is not always money that is being directed through a beneficiary designation. The word might be defined as anyone who receives a benefit from another after the giver's death. It could be money or an inheritance or even a gift. But there are various situations wherein a beneficiary is named along with various conditions or stipulations that might be involved with the designation. It might be a person or institution that is named as a potential recipient of money, such as a trust set up for a class of people—for example, the homeless or those suffering from a disease or illness.

It could be a gift or legacy left to others after the benefit has vested at the death of the giver. A group of unrelated and even unknown people could be the beneficiaries of another person or group or institution. For example, a city could install public bathrooms or bicycle trails and those who used them would be the beneficiaries who took advantage of the group or institution's actions. Humankind can be the beneficiary of medical advances or environmental protections. This book does not cover those broader categories of benefits that grantors bestow upon grantees. People and their relationships with other people in estate-planning situations are the areas I will explore. We also need to discuss the difference between revocable and irrevocable beneficiaries.

CHAPTER 2

Revocable and Irrevocable Beneficiaries

When planning for the distribution of assets after one's death, the choice between revocable and irrevocable beneficiaries can play a critical role in estate planning. Both types serve important functions but come with distinct advantages and disadvantages.

COMPARE AND CONTRAST

Revocable beneficiaries are individuals or entities named to receive assets from a financial account, insurance policy, or trust that can be changed or revoked by the account owner at any time before their death. So, revocable just means changeable. This flexibility allows individuals to adapt their estate plans to changing circumstances, such as marital status, financial situation, or relationships. Irrevocable beneficiaries are those which cannot be changed or removed without the beneficiary's consent. Once a beneficiary designation is set up as irrevocable, the account owner relinquishes control over that specific asset. This can provide certain advantages, such as asset protection and tax benefits, but limits the owner's ability to modify the designation.

Advantages of Revocable Beneficiaries

Flexibility: The primary advantage of revocable beneficiaries is the flexibility they provide. As life changes, account holders can adjust their beneficiaries accordingly. For example, if a beneficiary passes away or if the account holder enters into

7

a new relationship, changes can be made without significant legal hurdles.

Simplicity: Changes can often be made easily through a simple amendment form or available online account management. This ease of management can save time and reduce the potential for disputes among heirs.

Control: The account owner maintains control over the asset until their death, allowing them to make decisions that best fit their current situation.

Disadvantages of Revocable Beneficiaries

Potential for Misuse: Because revocable beneficiaries can be changed easily, there is a risk that the account holder might alter beneficiary designations impulsively, while impaired, or under undue influence, leading to family disputes and allegations of self-dealing or mismanagement.

Creditor Claims: Assets with revocable beneficiaries may still be considered part of the account holder's estate for creditor claims. This can pose a risk in situations where the account holder faces legal judgments or debts.

Advantages of Irrevocable Beneficiaries

Asset Protection: Assets designated to irrevocable beneficiaries are often shielded from creditors, as they are no longer considered part of the account holder's estate. This can be especially beneficial in protecting wealth from lawsuits or bankruptcy. Keep in mind, though, that there are statutes such as the Fraudulent Conveyance Act in some states, where transfers of assets to avoid creditor claims can be clawed back.

Tax Benefits: Certain irrevocable trusts can provide tax advantages, such as reducing the taxable estate or avoiding estate taxes altogether, depending on how they are structured.

Certainty and Security: Beneficiaries can feel secure knowing that their designation cannot be altered, which can prevent family disputes or confusion over asset distribution.

Medicaid Qualification: If you are creating a trust-based plan that preserves need-based programs for a beneficiary, the assets can be considered non-countable in determining eligibility for programs such as Medicaid or SSI, depending state law. The trust assets are also removed from the estate of the grantor of the trust, which can prove to be a tax benefit.

Disadvantages of Irrevocable Beneficiaries

Inflexibility: The inability to change the beneficiary can lead to complications if circumstances change. For example, if the irrevocable beneficiary dies or if the relationship with a grantee sours, the account holder has limited recourse to adjust the designation. However, with a carefully drawn plan, contingencies such as what to do in the event of the death of a beneficiary can be addressed when the documents are drafted. I call these the "what if?" scenarios that could reasonably occur, no matter how unlikely.

Complexity: Establishing irrevocable beneficiaries often requires more legal oversight and documentation, potentially leading to higher costs and more complicated estate planning processes.

Personal Circumstances: Life changes such as marriage, divorce, bankruptcy, or the birth of children and grandchildren can influence the decision to designate revocable or irrevocable beneficiaries. Understanding personal relationships and potential future changes is essential.

Financial Goals: If protecting assets from creditors or minimizing estate taxes is a priority, irrevocable beneficiaries may be more suitable. Conversely, if flexibility is more important, revocable beneficiaries may be the way to go.

Family Dynamics: Complex family situations, such as blended families or estranged relationships, can necessitate careful consideration of how beneficiaries are designated. The potential for disputes may make irrevocable designations less appealing.

Revocable Beneficiary Scenario

Consider a middle-aged individual, Alex, who has designated his sister as the revocable beneficiary on his life insurance policy. A few years later, Alex marries, and he wishes to update his beneficiary to include his new spouse for some or all of the insurance proceeds. The process is straightforward, and he submits a form to his insurance company, securing his spouse's future financial protection.

Irrevocable Beneficiary Scenario

Now, imagine Sarah, who has significant assets and wants to protect her wealth from potential creditors. She establishes an irrevocable trust, naming her children as beneficiaries. Although she cannot change this designation, it provides her peace of mind knowing her children's inheritance is safeguarded from her creditors, should any financial challenges arise.

Once you name someone as an irrevocable beneficiary, you generally cannot change the designation without their consent. This often applies in situations involving certain types of life insurance policies or trust arrangements. It also may be a requirement in a divorce decree to ensure the rights to alimony or child support. Sometimes, if allowed by the terms of an asset or insurance policy, the deceased might have sold his expected beneficiary benefit in life insurance, for example, to another person or company that would insist that the beneficiary change be made irrevocable to protect their investment.

Revocable Versus Irrevocable Trusts

Most trusts for estate planning purposes are revocable. That means that the trust maker—the grantor—can not only revoke the trust but can also change the terms of it by a simple amendment rather that starting from scratch. Once the grantor dies, the trust terms become irrevocable, i.e., unchangeable. But a trust can be set up so that some parts are unchangeable and other parts not. Also, a trust can by its terms continue for long after the death of the grantor for purposes such as managing money for a beneficiary for his or her life and may even continue for the lifetimes of the grantor's grandchildren. So, it is very flexible.

CHAPTER 3

If You Are the Grantor

Regardless of who you are, or how much money and property you have, your estate plan already exists. The plan is in effect right now, as you read this. You did not have to see a lawyer, make a will, set up a trust, or decide who gets what part of your assets at your death or who will be in charge of carrying out your plan.

WHO WILL BE YOUR BENEFICIARIES?

You see, if you do nothing at all, the law in your state of residence at the time of your death has already provided a plan for you. The plan is probably not what you would have chosen, but it is what it is and will stay that way if you die without having your plan in place.

I am talking about the written legal statutes that spell out the procedures to be used regarding your assets owned at death. The law abhors a vacuum, you see. So, if you die without a will or a trust, or have not named beneficiaries for your titled assets, your state law jumps in and sets out who gets what, when they get it, who oversees your estate, and the procedures that will be used to settle your estate. If you have not created documents to address these issues you are said to have died intestate—without a will.

Your estate will go through supervised probate if you rely on state law to determine your heirs. The laws are not exactly the same from state to state, but in general heirs are determined by your marital status; your children; and if no children a bloodline

13

chain of your grandchildren; your parents, if alive; siblings, if any; and if none of the above outlive you, then even nieces and nephews could be in line to inherit. At some point if there are no heirs in your familial chain, the assets in your name could escheat (or revert) to the state. So, the state of your residence becomes your beneficiary. For detailed and (we hope) accurate information in your state do an internet search for keywords "descent and distribution" + "your state's name."

A revocable trust is the best and most versatile basis for an estate plan. Aside from tax planning, there are at least eight situations where a trust is vital to carrying out the wishes of the deceased and providing long-term management of the trust assets for certain beneficiaries:

- A trust avoids probate if properly funded—a will must be probated.
- To protect and manage minor children's inheritance until their attaining the age of majority—or beyond.
- You have special needs or disabled heirs who depend upon need-based governmental programs.
- Your heirs are spendthrifts or are incarcerated or otherwise not able to manage their money properly.
- You and your partner are an unmarried couple. (Note that an unmarried couple can be any two or more unmarried persons. Mother and son, for example.)
- You and your partner and the children of each of you are a blended family, and you want to protect the inheritance rights of all the children.
- You and your partner have separate assets with different wishes as to who ultimately inherits. Note that you may choose separate trusts in that situation with separate trustees and separate beneficiary provisions.
- You want the privacy that a trust provides. Wills are public record so anyone can read your probate file and have access to what should be (in my opinion) private information.

A trust for estate planning purposes is much like a will. It lays out, in writing, who gets your assets at your death and under what conditions and names the people in charge of carrying out those instructions. The difference is that with a will all your assets are still in your name at your death and the heirs need a probate court order to transfer them to the heirs who are supposed to get them. Probate can cost thousands of dollars and take months or even years to complete. A trust is not required to go through probate.

The advantage of probate is that all of the actions of the probate personal representative can be under the supervision of the probate judge, which can be vital if the personal representative is less than honest or a sloppy record keeper.

A trust is similar to a corporation in that it is a legal entity created by paperwork as authorized by law and it has the ability to own things. For example, Ron's Doughnuts, Inc. is a corporation with a checking account, lots of ovens and display cases, dough mixers, donuts, and even a delivery truck. But Ron owns the corporation, so if Ron dies, the corporation is in a sense still alive and is still the owner of all the corporate assets. The corporate bylaws may direct what happens to the corporation insofar as management and control of the business are to be handled.

A trust is likewise a legal entity which can own things. Ron can create the trust and transfer the company assets into the trust name. So, Ron's trust can own Ron's house, his cars, his furniture, investments, and even the corporate stock in Ron's Doughnuts, Inc. When Ron dies, the trust is still alive and by its written instructions a new trust manager, called a trustee, takes over immediately to gather trust assets and disburse or manage them according to Ron's instructions.

All of this can be done with no lawyers or legal expense or waiting periods. The trust lawyer may create the trust document, but the post-death legal duties will be dramatically reduced. Remember that in a trust settlement, many of the actions taken are clerical in nature and do not require a lawyer to carry them out.

With a trust, the person in charge after your death can immediately begin carrying out your wishes with no court permission needed. Debts can be paid (there may be a waiting period on debt payment taking into account publication of the death of the trust creator and a time limit on presenting claims), assets transferred or sold, and when all the assets have been given out (or set aside for certain heirs such as minor children), the job is done. This typically takes a few weeks rather than years and involves little, if any, cost. Some states have state inheritance taxes that must be paid even though in most cases there is no federal estate tax. In those states a return must be filed for either a probate settlement or a probated will. The inheritance tax is usually only levied if the estate exceeds a certain minimum dollar amount.

The supposed downside of a trust is that it costs more than a will to set up. But the long-term cost savings and its flexibility are substantial with a trust. Also, there is a big disparity on what attorneys charge to create a trust-based estate plan. Some are reasonable and others are outrageously expensive—for what is basically the same situation. Shop around.

One not-uncommon situation is where a couple create a joint trust and put their assets into trust ownership. What once were individually owned assets have now become joint assets. Both parties could have originally agreed to a final distribution of all the assets, but the concern is that at the death of one of them, the survivor as sole trustee could change the revocable trust final distribution instructions. Many people who create a joint trust have children from a prior marriage and fear that the surviving grantor would remarry and leave the trust assets to a new spouse or would disinherit the first to die's heirs. Also if you are in a community property state (Arizona, California, Idaho, Louisiana, Nevada, New Mexico, Texas, Washington, and Wisconsin) or there are valid outstanding prenuptial agreements, an attorney should be consulted to see how that may affect the settlement process.

Question: My partner and I have been together for forty years but we have never married. Our house is mortgage free and it is in both of our names. We have joint bank accounts, and each own our own car. We have never talked about who our heirs should be since we are mostly concerned about taking care of each other. There were no children, but we do have siblings as well as nieces and nephews. Should we make a will?

My partner says the state law will decide who gets what when we are gone. I worry that there will be a lot of fighting and hurt feelings if nobody knows what we wanted done. Another thing: should we get married?

Answer: Settling an estate is the process of identifying and claiming your assets and your debts and, for sure under the eyes of a judge, seeing that all debts including court costs, taxes, and usually attorney fees are paid and that the remaining assets (if any) are turned over to the people who are legally entitled to them. My book *Settling Estates for Everyone* sets out in detail how to get through the process of gathering assets, paying expenses, and distributing those to the people entitled to them.

The government plan does not have to be your plan. If you want something different done, then it is up to you to put together a plan that satisfies your wishes and intentions. You need to create the plan before you become incompetent or die, since then it will in most cases be too late.

CHAPTER 4

Powers of Attorney

The very first step in protecting your assets should be to have a durable power of attorney prepared that gives a person you choose the ability to handle your affairs, including the power to create a will or trust if you become incapable of doing it yourself. Who can be your agent under a power of attorney? Usually, it is the trustee of your trust or a beneficiary of the estate or even a family member. It cannot be someone who is developmentally disabled, or a minor, or someone who is incarcerated or institutionalized. I don't recommend naming your lawyer, although you can in most states. But even so, you cannot name your lawyer as a beneficiary in most cases.

CREATE ONE NOW, NOT LATER

What is a power of attorney? Basically, it is a written permission slip for someone to sign your name and make business-type decisions for you. Your agent (sometimes called your "attorney-in-fact") would have the legal ability to sign on your behalf (you are the "principal") for such things as property management, tax returns, investment decisions, or any other transaction that the principal could normally do if not disabled. Some of these documents only take legal effect if you, the principal, are unable to act for yourself. We call that a "springing" power since it specifically requires a finding of mental or physical incapacity by either a medical professional or two. This type of power can give wide authority over nearly any transaction in which the principal might be involved.

A power of attorney can be limited in time—basically having an expiration date—or be limited to certain types of transactions. As an example, the principal might need to have someone stand in for her in a real estate or business deal. This would be a limited power since it would specify what the agent is empowered to do and would only be good for that particular transaction. It might also give the agent the ability to arrange the deposit of funds from the transaction to the principal's financial institution.

A power of attorney might also set out things that an agent may not do. Usually, we do not give the agent the power to change or rescind a will, trust, or beneficiary designation. But in a case where the principal is incapacitated and the agent is a family member, we may allow that power. Sometimes the principal wants the agent to have unlimited power, so make your intentions clear when you talk to your attorney about the power of attorney.

People ask me why they can't just use a power of attorney to set things up correctly and follow their instructions for paying bills, using credit cards, cashing checks, and so forth after a person dies. The reason is that the POA document is invalid after the death of the principal. So, it is too late to redo a will or trust after a person dies. Most often, the rule is that after death the trust or will becomes irrevocable, that is, it's unchangeable. Complicating this answer is the possible existence of so-called powers of appointment contained in a will or trust, where a successor trustee or personal representative has the specific authority to make changes to the will or trust for tax savings or other specific reasons.

But in any event the power of attorney cannot be used for any other purpose after the person dies. This makes sense since the POA gives the agent the power to do what the principal could otherwise do.

Avoiding probate can be done for two important situations. Not putting your estate through the estates division of the probate court is one. Another division of the probate court concerns the need for adult guardianship and conservatorship proceedings. This is used when a person is in fact mentally incompetent but who has no power of attorney. Since she is incompetent, it is too late for her to appoint someone as her medical and business agent, so the court must appoint someone for the job.

The court process to do this can be expensive, time-consuming, and in some cases embarrassing to the incompetent person. Family members, her physician, and a court-appointed ad litem visiting attorney may have to testify as to specifically what she has done to need a conservator or guardian. This would be done in open court and could be contested. And the judge may even question her.

Get a power of attorney while you still can.

A power of attorney is basically a document that allows someone to legally act for another in business transactions. The POA can be revoked, that is cancelled, at any time by the person giving the power. Similarly, the agent has the right to resign. If you had two or more people named as agents and the first choice declines, the alternate would take over and sign an acceptance of duties. Since you are giving your agent the right to act for you, after your death you have no ability to sign documents or enter into contracts and so the power of attorney is instantly invalid at your death. If you can't sign a document, then neither can your agent.

But what if you are not dead but are instead disabled to the extent that you cannot manage your own affairs? In normal cases that would mean your agent has no more power than you do and so the power of attorney is invalid unless you regain competency. But a power of attorney can be written so that it continues to be valid even in the event of incompetency. We call that a durable power of attorney because it survives disability.

Question: My father recently died after suffering from dementia for several years. He had a revocable trust and a durable power of attorney naming my oldest brother, Bill, as his trustee and agent under the POA. His estate was worth about three million dollars before the onset of the disease, and for the balance of his life Bill used the POA to pay his bills and manage his investments. Now Bill says that there is less than one million left in the accounts. I found out Bill was using the money to pay his own personal expenses in addition to those of my father. He bought himself a car, saying he needed it to take Dad to medical appointments, but also paid himself a salary for acting as his caregiver for several years. He has no receipts for anything and did not keep any kind of expense log but says all his expenditures were legitimate. He also used some money to put a small addition on his house so Dad could have a private bedroom and bath.

The question is what can I do to try to recover money that I think was inappropriately removed from my dad's trust assets? It is a trust, so Bill says it was entirely up to him as to spending and he has no intention of accounting for what he did. Do I have any recourse? There are three other siblings besides the two of us, but they all say leave well enough alone.

Answer: All is not lost. There actually is something you can do. The trustee and POA agent-in-fact has a fiduciary duty to take care of the money in the estate and make appropriate investments and expenditures. Bill was obviously engaged in what lawyers call self-dealing. He used at least some of the money for his own primary benefit, not the benefit of your father.

I suggest filing for the probate of his estate and asking the court to order an itemized accounting of all expenditures. You could also ask that you, or some other person, be appointed the Personal Representative of the estate to manage the remaining funds in the trust before they get misappropriated. The addition to his house absolutely benefitted Bill more than your father, particularly in the long run since it likely increased the value of

Bill's property at the expense of the trust assets. Get a lawyer who is experienced in probate litigation. I think you have a good case.

Consult the Appendix to see the rather severe penalties that a court can impose on someone violating their fiduciary duty. This is a Michigan statute, but similar laws exist in most other states.

CHAPTER 5

Trustees and Trust Directors

The trust director (in some jurisdictions called a trust protector) is the person named in a trust whose duty is to protect and supervise the rights of the trust beneficiaries. The director is named to carry out the intent of the trust grantor, and to remove or replace a trustee for cause. Cause includes such things as mishandling of trust assets, self-dealing, and failing to follow the clear intent of the grantor. In some states there are statutes that allow the use of different trustees for different roles in administering the trust.

There can be in a complex trust the following types of trustees with differing duties:

1. A investment trustee, which might be a bank.
2. A directed trustee, who acts at the direction of the trust director.
3. A distributions trustee, who could be a family member responsible for carrying out distributions to trust beneficiaries.
4. A resultant trustee, who would be in charge of all trust actions not under the control of the other trustees.

A trust director, a.k.a. trust protector, could be a disinterested person (meaning not a beneficiary) who oversees the trustees and has the legal authority to replace them if need be. The powers of the trust protector are set out in the language of the trust document. The idea is to ensure that the trustees are acting as fiduciaries for the benefit of the grantor's heirs. While a trust is normally irrevocable at the death or disability of the grantors, with a trust protector the trust can be modified by the trust protector if necessary to carry out the wishes of the original grantors. The compensation of the trust protector is also spelled out in the trust document. This role has to be set up in advance of the grantor's death, so this includes the powers and duties of the trust protector.

The trust protector role is not often called for in a typical family joint trust with non-substantial assets. The primary purpose of a typical family trust may be more probate avoidance and not so much managing a trust with complex distribution plans, varied asset types, or management of trusts that are intended to exist for the lifetime of some or all beneficiaries.

The role of a trust protector is to provide an additional layer of oversight and protection for a trust. Trust protectors are typically appointed by the grantor (the person who establishes the trust) and have certain powers and responsibilities outlined in the trust instrument. Their primary duty is to act in the best interests of the beneficiaries and ensure that the trust is managed and administered properly.

Here are some key roles and responsibilities of a trust protector:

Monitoring and Oversight: Trust protectors have the authority to monitor the actions of the trustee(s) and ensure they are acting in accordance with the terms of the trust. They can review financial statements, investment decisions, and other relevant information to ensure compliance.

Trust Modification or Amendment: In certain situations, a trust protector may have the power to modify or amend the trust provisions. This power is usually granted to allow adjustments in response to changing circumstances or to address unforeseen events.

Removal and Replacement of Trustees: Trust protectors can have the authority to remove and replace trustees if they determine that the current trustee is not fulfilling their duties properly or if there are conflicts of interest. This power helps to ensure that the trust's administration remains in capable hands.

Resolving Disputes: In case of conflicts or disputes arising within the trust, a trust protector may be empowered to resolve these issues impartially. They can act as a mediator or arbitrator to find fair and equitable solutions.

Safeguarding Beneficiary Interests: Trust protectors are responsible for safeguarding the interests of the trust beneficiaries. They must act in their best interests and protect against any potential mismanagement, abuse, or undue influence.

Acting as a Successor Trustee: In some cases, a trust protector may be designated as a successor trustee who steps in to administer the trust if the original trustee is unable or unwilling to fulfill their duties.

It's important to note that the specific powers and responsibilities of a trust protector can vary depending on the terms outlined in the trust agreement. Therefore, it's crucial to carefully review the trust instrument to understand the exact role and authority granted to the trust protector in each particular case.

CHAPTER 6

Fairness in Naming Heirs

Deciding what is "fair" when it comes to determining inheritance is a highly personal and subjective matter. There is no one-size-fits-all answer, as it depends on your individual circumstances, values, and priorities. Here are some factors and considerations to keep in mind when making these decisions in your estate planning:

Family Dynamics: Consider the dynamics within your family, including second marriages, stepchildren, and any existing tensions or conflicts. Open communication and transparency can help address concerns and avoid disputes later.

Spousal Rights: In many jurisdictions, spouses have legal rights to a portion of the estate, regardless of what is stated in a will. This right is called an election against the will and can defeat a plan to disinherit their partner by demanding a statutory share rather than what the will provided. Make sure to understand the laws in your area and account for your spouse's needs and rights after your death.

Special Needs Heirs: If you have a disabled or special-needs heir, it's usually considered essential to plan for their long-term financial well-being. Special needs trusts can be created to provide for them without jeopardizing their eligibility for government assistance.

Minors: If you have minor children, consider appointing a guardian in your will to ensure they are cared for if you and your spouse are unable to do so. You can also set up trusts to manage their inheritance until they reach a certain age or satisfy criteria you set up before they can receive their inheritance.

Assets from Previous Marriages: If you or your spouse bring assets into the marriage, it's important to clarify whether these assets should remain separate or become part of the joint estate. A prenuptial or postnuptial agreement can help with this. If you live in a community property state, assets and debts are shared equally unless you follow the rules regarding separately owned or jointly owned assets.

Equal vs. Fair: Keep in mind that "fair" doesn't always mean "equal." Depending on individual circumstances and needs, it may be fair to distribute assets unequally among heirs. Justification for these decisions may include the needs of beneficiary, his or her record of mismanagement of finances, or even such things as a grantor's dislike of the potential heir or his or her spouse. It's your money so you can do whatever you want, without having to explain the reasons for your decisions.

Consider Professional Advice: Consult with an estate planning attorney or financial adviser to help you navigate complex situations and ensure that your wishes are legally documented.

Regularly Update Your Plan: Life circumstances change, so it's crucial to revisit your estate plan periodically, especially after major life events such as marriages, divorces, births, or deaths.

Discuss with Family: While you may not be required to discuss your estate plan with your family, open and honest conversations can help manage expectations and minimize potential conflicts. But, again, remember your decisions are private and no one but you has the right to decide whether your plan is fair or not.

Personal Values: Consider your own values, beliefs, and priorities when making these decisions. You may want to leave a portion of your estate to charitable causes or organizations that are meaningful to you. Equal distribution of assets among heirs is often the default choice, but it may not always be the fairest option. Consider the unique needs and circumstances of each family member. Some may have financial stability, while others may need more assistance. To avoid conflicts, consider an equitable distribution that takes individual needs into account rather than simply dividing assets equally.

Appointing a Neutral Executor or Trustee: Selecting an unbiased and neutral executor can help maintain peace within the family. An executor's role is to ensure that the deceased's wishes are carried out as per the will or the legal requirements. When a family member is chosen as the executor, it may raise suspicions of bias. Opting for a neutral third party, such as a financial adviser or a lawyer, can minimize conflicts and ensure an impartial distribution process.

Emotions in Check: Dealing with the loss of a loved one is an emotionally charged experience, and emotions can run high during asset distribution discussions. It's crucial for all family members to recognize the emotional aspect of the situation and make an effort to keep emotions in check. Encourage empathy and understanding among heirs, and remind them that the goal is to honor the deceased's wishes and maintain family unity.

Determining what is fair in terms of bequests in a will and trust is subjective and dependent on various factors. There is no true fairness since no two situations in family relationships and asset owners are alike. Here are some considerations that can help guide you in deciding what may be considered fair:

Individual Circumstances: Take into account the personal circumstances of each beneficiary, including their financial needs, existing assets, and their relationship with the testator (the person creating the will or trust). For example, if one beneficiary is financially stable while another is in significant need, you may consider adjusting the bequests accordingly.

Testator's Intent: Consider the wishes and intentions of the testator as expressed in the will or trust. The testator's desires should be given considerable weight when determining what is fair, as long as they are legally valid and not influenced by undue pressure or duress.

Equal Treatment: Fairness often involves treating beneficiaries equally, especially in the absence of specific reasons for unequal distribution. Many people choose to divide their estate equally among their beneficiaries to avoid potential conflicts or perceived favoritism.

Special Circumstances: Some beneficiaries may have special needs, disabilities, or require ongoing financial support. In such cases, it may be fair to allocate a larger portion of the estate to meet their specific requirements.

Consider any contributions or sacrifices made by specific beneficiaries during the testator's lifetime. This could include emotional support, caregiving, financial assistance, or other significant efforts that may warrant a larger bequest.

Be aware of any legal obligations or requirements imposed by local laws. Some jurisdictions have laws that protect certain family members from being completely disinherited, and failing to comply with these laws may lead to legal challenges.

If conflicts arise that cannot be resolved through open communication, consider seeking professional mediation. A trained mediator can facilitate discussions and help family members find common ground. Mediation can be a cost-effective and efficient way to resolve disputes and maintain family harmony.

To prevent future disputes and ensure transparency, keep meticulous records of all asset distribution decisions and transactions. This includes documenting the deceased's will, any changes or amendments, and records of asset transfers. Clear documentation can serve as evidence of the fairness and legality of the distribution process.

Preventing conflicts in the future begins with proactive estate planning. Encourage your loved ones to regularly review and update their estate plans to reflect changes in their assets, family dynamics, and wishes. This proactive approach can help avoid surprises and conflicts down the road.

Include provisions for managing your assets and making healthcare decisions in the event of your incapacity. Durable powers of attorney and healthcare proxy documents are essential to give your family the authority to help you if you are physically or mentally unable to do things for yourself. Explore strategies to minimize estate taxes and other tax liabilities, such as gifting, charitable contributions, and utilizing tax-efficient accounts.

CHAPTER 7

The Family Cottage: Solutions to Joint Ownership Problems

Whether its's called a cottage, a camp, a cabin, or the family vacation property, while easily shareable during Mom and Dad's lifetime, it can become a difficult thing to keep in the family once the parents are gone. Now it is a matter of money.

The family cottage as an inherited property often creates a lot of family dissension. While the parents are alive there is no issue, and the parents think that the cottage should stay in the family since everyone had fond memories of their days at the lake. But after the death of the parents, the family dynamics usually change, sometimes fueled by in-laws who had no history with the property. It becomes an asset with expenses but no return. So it becomes all about money.

The co-owners of the cottage are equally liable for expenses and equally entitled to its use. Knowing this, the solution to be considered is a family partnership agreement combined with a buyout for those who want to sell. If you inherited the property recently, there would be little capital gains tax for those who get bought out because they get a stepped-up tax basis as of the date of the inheritance.

There are some other solutions that could be brought to the table. It could be treated it as a time-share with an agreement as to how many weeks and during which months each party owns. Would the joint owners be able to rent their weeks to the general public by using a vacation rental company?

That method would give the non-users a way of profiting from their share so they would have no out-of-pocket expenses and in fact would make money on it. Others could use it for some or all of their weeks with the property expenses coming out of their rental income for some of their weeks. Once a year or so the weeks could be switched around so that one owner would not end up with the least desirable weeks.

There is also the possibility of the ones who want to keep it buying out the others if their finances allow that. The buyers then could make their own agreement as to use and maintenance of the property.

This problem is so prevalent that there are now standard form contracts to create trusts for the inheritance of vacation property. These so-called "cottage trusts" retain the ownership after the death of the original owners and sometimes provide a fund from which the cottage expenses are paid in the future. The respective uses of the property by the beneficiaries are laid out and provisions are included to allow the grandchildren to continue as trust beneficiaries entitled to the use of the property. You can even include a mechanism for dissolving the trust if the trust beneficiaries agree, since none of us know what the future will be insofar as the desires of future generations.

A similar problem is the disposition of the family home. Should it be sold and the proceeds added to the trust disposition? What if one or more of the heirs is still living in the house? Does that person want the house as part or all of his share of the inheritance? If he wants the house, are there enough other assets that would have enough value to equally cover the other heirs' share? Does the house have a mortgage that must be paid before title can be transferred or the property sold? Would it make sense to put the house in the names of all the heirs and rent it? Those questions and more must be resolved as part of the trust distribution.

CHAPTER 8

Trusting Your Trustee

If you are using a trust as the basis for your estate planning, it is vitally important that you can rely on your trustee's honesty and efficiency. Certainly, we don't want to see a trustee steal from the trust or invest the trust assets in high-risk investments. There are several ways to protect your trust assets from being poorly invested or even embezzled.

It is unusual to see a named trustee deliberately self-deal and take money from the trust for his or her own use. Sometimes it is not intentional theft but merely poor decision making that leads to trouble. As an heir or beneficiary, you want to be sure you receive regular accountings as to the trust funds. How much was spent, to whom money was paid, and the purpose of the payment should all be regularly relayed to you as an heir.

While the grantors of the trust are alive and mentally competent, the grantors acting as their own trustees are not required to give you, as a potential heir, any accountings of trust assets. The reason is that you are not vested as an heir. The grantors can change the trust at any time and that includes changing who will ultimately inherit. It is only when the grantors die or are deemed incompetent that the trust becomes irrevocable and therefore unchangeable that the heirs become vested in their share of the trust assets and are then entitled to periodic accountings.

Naming co-trustees is a good way to be sure the trust is being managed competently and honestly. Having two or more trustees working together requires that they all participate in all decisions as to expenditures and investments. So, they in effect police each other and it is unlikely that there will be any problems with illegal or unethical behavior.

Hiring a professional trustee from a bank or trust company is another way to protect the trust. The problem with this method is that most banks and trust companies require a large minimum amount of trust funds before they will take on the role of trustee.

Estate planning is more than signing papers to create a will or trust. Before any of that can happen, decisions must be made. First, decide what type of plan would best suit your needs as well as the needs of your family or heirs. There are tax considerations for some of you and minimizing the tax cost can be extremely important for high asset estates. Since the federal estate tax exemption amount has increased recently, most estates will not be subject to that tax. However, a number of states have now increased their inheritance tax, which can be an important planning consideration for some estates.

If there is no named professional trustee or trust company helping administer the settlement of an estate, the job is usually the responsibility of one or more family members. The idea of making the children co-trustees working together solves a couple of problems.

First, they can split up the duties so that everything doesn't fall into the lap of just one person. If there was just one trustee and things drag on, the other heirs may second-guess the decisions of the sole trustee and decide to hire their own attorney. That is almost always a bad idea.

Second, when there is more than one trustee, perhaps even three or four, the signing of documents becomes burdensome since they would all have to sign off on everything.

On the other hand, if there are named trustees who have varying specific skills, the duties can be divided among them according to their qualifications. Or if they are all capable but some have work or business obligations, those might be let off the hook and the others could handle everything. Same for those who do not live in the geographic area of the person's death.

Question: I have been named as a co-trustee along with my two brothers for my father's trust. My mother passed away several years ago and now my father has also died. The problem is that his estate was very diverse, with a vacation home in another state, lots of investments, and two houses full of furniture and personal property, some of which has been handed down from earlier generations. It looks like most everything is in the trust so no probate would be needed. The issue is that we don't get along and have been estranged for some time. It is difficult to even talk to one another and we mostly use email and messaging. I can't imagine how we are going to work together to settle this estate. What are our options?

Answer: Perhaps this is exactly why he made you co-trustees. Maybe his plan was to force you to work together to reach some sort of rapprochement. Remember that this is a one-time situation with an end in sight. Set aside past differences at least temporarily so that the job can be done quickly and inexpensively for everyone's benefit.

But what if that is just not possible? I suggest appointing a third party to act on behalf of the trust to settle the estate. If there is no one you can all agree on I suggest hiring a professional mediator who also deals in estates. Mediators are usually attorneys who are familiar with the legal process as well as resolving differences of expectations among diverse groups.

The agreement with the mediator should be in writing, laying out the scope of his or her duties. The end result may be a recommendation as to how to dispose of the estate assets or may include a hands-on management of the process itself. If that doesn't work, you can rely on the courts. While we try to

(Continued...)

keep people out of probate if at all possible, any one of the three of you can petition the court for supervision of the trust. The court would likely appoint a public administrator to carry out the distribution instructions of the trust, thereby superseding the co-trustee arrangement. The court might also appoint just one of you as acting trustee. It's not a bad idea if you offer the judge suggestions as to acceptable solutions.

Question: I have been named as the sole personal representative of my mother's will. My four siblings are also heirs along with me. My sister's husband is a banker and thinks he knows more than the rest of us—especially me, since I never went to college. Can they replace me as trustee with him? I haven't done anything wrong and am just trying to get the whole process over without them telling me what to do.

Answer: This is a common problem under the heading of conflict resolution. The death of a loved one is one of the most stressful and depressing events in a person's life. We all deal with the loss of a loved one in different ways. Some reactions are apparent to all and some you will bever know about. Anger, lashing out, depression, denial, all can be present at time of death so don't take it personally. It's easy to be defensive if your actions or decisions are second-guessed. The best thing to do is be patient and understand that people may exhibit behavior that is out of character. They may be subject to influences from their spouses or children that magnify their own behavior toward the person in charge of the estate as well as the other heirs.

It may be that they had their own conception as to how things were to be done even though that conception is at odds with what the deceased might have wanted or specifically directed in the language of the will or trust. Remember that a year or two from now this estate will be final and all the issues sorted. Patience and understanding are key for all involved. The estate procedures last for a finite time while the relationship with your family goes on.

Above all, do not let them replace you if you want the job. There was a reason you were appointed, and it might boil down to your mother's faith in your integrity and honesty. It's easy to let them bulldoze you, but you likely have an attorney, at least on a consulting basis who can act as intermediary if necessary. But the main thing you can do is provide complete disclosure and transparency with what you are doing.

Often the family is not aware of the time requirements and the complexity of the probate procedures. A group meeting with the estate lawyer can be a big help in tempering people's expectations. The lawyer can go over filing requirements, notices required to creditors, tax filing issues, mandatory waiting periods, the need for appraisals, and other procedural tasks that must be undertaken. They are less likely to think that they need their own lawyers (which invariably increases the expense and time of the probate process). You must keep them informed but they need to understand that the decisions being made are yours to make and not a majority-rules sort of situation.

Of course, if you or your attorney are not acting as fiduciaries and are not doing what is best for the heirs as a whole, or are involved in self-dealing, then they have reason to complain and can even petition the court to have you removed. Stay strong, do the right thing, and this will all be over one day.

Question: Even though I was named executor of my best friend's will, I don't really want the job. We were close, but I don't know her family and am not listed as one of her heirs. I have my own life to deal with. Can I appoint someone else who has a family connection or at least more time to spend on the estate?

Answer: No. you cannot appoint someone else if you don't want the job. Usually, a will names a first choice as executor (personal

(Continued ...)

representative) but also names a second or even third choice in the event the first choice dies or does not want to do it. Since it is a probate situation, paperwork would have to be filed with the court for you to decline to serve and the court would then appoint the next person in line. If no one wants to do it then the court can appoint a public administrator (usually an attorney) to be the executor—who, of course, has to be paid from the estate assets.

The same answer holds if the estate is in a trust, except that the only time a judge is involved is if there is no one who wants the job of trustee. In most states, the probate court has the authority to act in a limited manner for a trust issue without turning it into a full-blown probate case; so, naming a substitute trustee is within their authority. But read the trust carefully since a well-written trust will have directives on how a trustee can be selected without recourse to a court proceeding. For example, it may state that if there is no one named who is willing or able to act as trustee, the majority of beneficiaries can choose a trustee. But first, let's briefly revisit the required or desired process to settle the legal affairs of the deceased person's estate.

CHAPTER 9

Ignoring the Wishes of the Deceased

When can you legally ignore the instructions, trustee appointment, or distribution plans set out in a will or trust? Presumably the decedent put some thought and reasoning behind his or her decisions and it would seem somehow wrong to change those directives. Unless everyone agrees. No harm no foul.

IS THAT EVEN LEGAL?

Most of the time when a person makes a will or trust the planned distribution of assets follows normal patterns. A married couple will most often want to leave everything to each other, and at the death of a survivor they would want to divide the remaining estate equally among their children. The survivor typically has the right to make changes to the will or trust but usually doesn't do that. However, circumstances can, and often do, cause a person to want to change their original desires. For example, children sometimes become at odds with their parents due to lifestyle, addictions, criminal involvement, relationships that parents find objectionable, and many other reasons causing estrangement between parents and children.

Sometimes changing a will to eliminate a child as an heir makes sense. If an heir is incarcerated or institutionalized, an inheritance would do little good and would likely not benefit the heir. All potential heirs need to understand that they are not legally entitled to anything just because they are related to the deceased. While it is true that if there is no will the laws direct that the person's closest relatives are legally entitled to inherit the person's assets, those who make wills and trusts sometimes feel guilty about omitting or limiting an inheritance and in an effort to be fair may make decisions that do not necessarily conflate with their actual desires.

The best-intentioned people sometimes create an estate plan that results in drama, dissention, resentment, and even fistfights among their heirs. Maybe there is only one valuable antique china cabinet that more than one heir is expecting to inherit. It's not just money that heirs are competing for; it could be who gets the family business, family heirlooms, or the classic sports car. If the expectations of the family are not in line with the directives of the deceased, there is often resentment or hurt feelings, if not more serious repercussions. This does not have to happen if everyone can get on board with a reasonable way of dividing up all the personal property stuff that is not exactly as spelled out in the will or trust.

I have seen several examples of how to handle this. One father decided to leave great-grandfather's double-barrel shotgun to one of the sons because he thought that son wanted it. The son liked it but knew that his brother was actually the one who cherished the gun and so handed it over to his brother, who happily hung it over his fireplace. That gesture kept the brother-to-brother relationship solid with no worry of resentment on the part of the gun's new owner. We hope that kind of gesture could be the rule rather than the exception.

Trading things back and forth is okay, of course, if all those involved agree. Sometimes, though, people make assumptions as to who should get what and fairness does not prevail. A way of handling personal property division is first to make an inventory of everything (within reason) in the estate and let the heirs list the things they would like to have, then compare the lists. If one heir's list is weighted with all the desirable or valuable items, it is easy for everyone to see that, and adjustments can be made. If it seems impossible to get items sorted by agreement, then items can be chosen by lot. Each person would take turns

Ignoring the Wishes of the Deceased 45

choosing one item and then the next one would be in line to make a choice in a round-robin fashion, with the instruction that the heirs should try to keep the total value of their choices approximately equal. I have seen people decide that daughters-in-law and sons-in-laws are not to participate in this process. The estate attorney could supervise this if need be.

If it is just impossible to get an agreement among the heirs, and the will or trust is not specific about who gets which tangible assets, then the probate court can direct a system of division. I once had a case where the two heirs were fighting over Dad's golf clubs and refused to agree or take something else of equal value. The judge did the King Solomon method by declaring that one brother got the putter and the 3, 4, and 5 irons as well as the 3 and 5 woods and the other brother got the rest of the set plus the golf bag. Realizing that following the judge's order would be of no value to either of them, they made a trade for another item and one brother got the whole set.

Leaving the decision to a judge is not the best idea.

CHAPTER 10

The Family Business

According to the Small Business Administration, there are about 33 million small businesses in the United States as of the time of this writing. A small business is defined as one that is independently owned and operated and has fewer than 1,500 employees. However, only ten percent actually employ more than 100 employees. The total value of these businesses is in the billions of dollars. At some point all these business owners die and their ownership interest is passed on to their heirs or partners.

SELL IT OR KEEP IT?

Succession planning is a legal and financial specialty utilizing the skills of lawyers, accountants, financial planners, and insurance companies. Their goal is to see that at the death of the owners a business continues to operate with the value of the business being transferred to the heirs of the owner with the least hassle and expense possible. It is heavily involved in identifying critical roles in the management and operation of a company and attempting to fill those roles prior to or shortly after the death or retirement of the owners.

For our purposes, we are concerned about succession planning before and after death as an estate planning tool and developing a plan that will take care of the families of the deceased so as to avoid conflict and legal problems from competing heirs. The planning should start now. Once a key person has died the legal and personal quagmire begins, if careful planning had not been done.

If the business is a partnership, the partners absolutely need a written partnership agreement. Here are the factors to consider:

What will happen to the share of a partner if he dies? One thing most partners do not want is to have the family of the deceased partner try to take over his or her place in the business. Do they have the desire to take over the deceased partners role? More importantly, do they have the skills needed to fill that role? Does the surviving partner want a new partner who may or may not be suited to helping run the business? The partnership agreement should address the issue of the death of a partner.

If a buyout of the deceased partner's interest is desired, then there needs to be a way of valuing that share as well as a plan to fund the buyout. Typically, partners will purchase reciprocal life insurance policies payable on death to the business so that the proceeds of the insurance can be used to fund the buyout. Insurance agents are familiar with that type of policy and the premium payments are a legitimate business expense.

Methods of valuing the buyout are important since most businesses have more than just inventory, real estate, and fixtures to be valued. There may be contracts, liabilities, lawsuits, goodwill, and intangible investments in the business name. These all are counted as pluses and minuses in determining value. The agreement may require the services of a professional business appraiser to be used when the need to come up with a number arises.

Another valuable point to consider, depending upon the type of business involved, is the value of a customer list. In one case the surviving partner did not want to deal with the family of the dead partner. Instead of buying out the partner's share he closed the business, offering to turn over the inventory, equipment, and fixtures to the family, and re-opened a month later under another name and in another location after soliciting the customer list of the original business. The value of the business was in its relationship with the customer base, so the survivor in effect got the lion's share of the business assets for very little cost to himself.

It goes without saying that there was no partnership agreement in that case.

Other things to consider are obligations to employees under employment agreements, IRS withholding, workers compensation expenses, ongoing lawsuits, tax deposits, and accounts payable and receivable. You need a business attorney to navigate the sale or assignment of a family small business.

But it's not just death that needs to be accounted for. What if a partner becomes disabled, develops dementia, or wants to retire? What happens if a partner declares bankruptcy, or is involved in a divorce action, or is imprisoned? All partners should be barred from assigning, selling, or borrowing against their share in the business without the consent of all co-owners. And there needs to be a clearly defined exit strategy for someone who wants out.

Are there any family members involved in the business as owners or employees? They might be suitable candidates to take over management of the company. If the company is a partnership, are the family members of the deceased partner protected? Should they be given employment contracts? Are any of them interested in or capable of operating the business?

There are some businesses in which the value depends almost entirely on the direct labor of the business owner. This type might not be saleable except for the value of inventory, real estate, and equipment. These might include a skilled glass blower, artist, entertainer, cabinet maker, or auto mechanic. A freelance-type worker, working with few or no employees, can still prepare his or her estate for liquidation by transferring all titled assets, such as vehicles, real estate, and watercraft, into a revocable trust so that these items need not go through probate.

Okay, so we know what planning should be done before the death of the family business owner. But what can be done after the person's death if no planning had taken place? That depends upon the type of business. Let's look at a multi-generational family farm.

Suppose there is a family business such as a farm, which has real estate, crops in the field, and farm equipment as its assets. And suppose there are several children who are heirs of the deceased farmer but only one who works full-time operating the farming business. How can the estate be divided fairly among all the children and still keep the farm as an ongoing business which requires the management of the child working the farm? The farmland has value, of course, but dividing up the land or selling it would mean the business would have to be shut down. That might be the last thing the deceased farmer wanted to happen.

If there are other assets that can be passed on to the non-farming children, then that might solve the unequal distribution problem. One case that I handled had a large farm being run by the father and one son. There were two other children who had long-term careers in other areas, and they had no desire to take over even part of the farm operation. But they did want their share of the estate. On the property were several barns and outbuildings and numerous pieces of farm equipment. Crops were in the ground but not quite ready to harvest. There was a large family farmhouse where the father had lived and another brick house down the road that was being used as a rental.

We valued the land based on its use as farmland and added the value of the tools and equipment. Both houses were appraised separately. In the end the farmer son got the land, including the barns, and the houses were sold with the sale proceed going to the other siblings. That arrangement still left the farmer son with about sixty percent of the total asset value, so he entered into an agreement to pay his siblings enough to balance out the shares in the form of a mortgage to them over a period of years. Everyone was happy and the farm stayed in the family.

Selling the family business is usually a way of settling that part of the estate. Someone in the family might wish to buy the others out. The only sticking points might be the price to be paid and when that payment can be made.

Business brokers are familiar with sales of businesses, of course, and have contacts who can assist in the transfer. Sometimes a sale requires approval of a licensing authority, such as a liquor control commission in the case of a retail store or restaurant selling and/or serving liquor. Similar approvals might be needed for a drugstore or a gambling establishment. The health department may have to approve the equipment and premises of a food store or medical office. The business broker will know how to apply for and get those approvals. Their fees are typically a percentage of the sale price plus the fees for inventory companies, accountants, lawyers, and other service professionals.

It is important to keep the business in operation if possible. A going business will sell more quickly and for a better price than one which has been shut down. There is an advantage to having some employees carry over from one owner to another. Competitors in the same business may also be a good source for a buyout.

One idea that could work if the family wants to keep the business but also wants access to cash to settle the estate is a so-called sale and lease back. This is when the family reaches an agreement to sell the real estate and buildings of the business and also agrees to rent it from the new buyer for a term of years with a possible agreement to allow them the first right of refusal if the building is to be re-sold. An investor might find this more desirable than a straight sale since a vacant building might be harder to rent and rent for less money than with an existing tenant. A stepped-up tax basis for capital gains purposes on the inherited building will assist the seller/heirs as well.

For businesses selling products on credit, the accounts receivable list is an asset that can be sold as well. If you are making the succession plan, be sure your heirs know how to access all your accounts including those online. This would be things like usernames and passwords. If you use cryptocurrency such as Bitcoin, it is very important that your account information is available to your probate executor or trustee so that these accounts are not abandoned.

Include provisions for managing your assets and making healthcare decisions in the event of your incapacity. Durable powers of attorney and healthcare proxy documents are often used for this purpose and are described earlier in this book.

Review and update your will and trust documents periodically, especially after major life events such as marriages, divorces, births, or significant changes in your financial situation.

Explore strategies to minimize estate taxes and other tax liabilities, such as gifting, charitable contributions, and utilizing tax-efficient accounts.

CHAPTER 11

Special Needs Trusts

Medicaid trusts are specialized financial instruments designed to help individuals qualify for Medicaid benefits while protecting their assets. As Medicaid is a critical program for low-income individuals needing expensive or long-term care, understanding the role and mechanics of Medicaid trusts is essential for effective financial and estate planning.

MEDICAID QUALIFICATION AND ASSET MANAGEMENT

Medicaid is a needs-based program funded in part by the federal government and administered by the states, primarily designed to assist individuals with limited income and resources to get medical care. For many, especially the elderly requiring long-term care, the cost of services can be overwhelming. Medicaid trusts serve several purposes:

Asset Protection: By placing assets into a properly drawn trust, individuals can potentially reduce their countable assets for Medicaid eligibility.

Income Preservation: Trusts can help preserve income for the benefit of the individual or their heirs, ensuring that essential needs are met without jeopardizing Medicaid eligibility.

Estate Planning: Medicaid trusts can facilitate a smoother transfer of assets upon death, often bypassing probate and minimizing estate taxes.

Beneficiary Guide for Everyone

Care Management: For individuals with long-term care needs, trusts can be structured to ensure funds are used specifically for their care.

IRREVOCABLE MEDICAID TRUSTS

Irrevocable Medicaid trusts are the most commonly used type for Medicaid planning. Once assets are transferred into this trust, the individual grantor creating the trust cannot alter the trust terms or reclaim the assets. Key features include:

Asset Exclusion: Assets placed in an irrevocable trust are generally not counted towards Medicaid's asset limit, which can help individuals qualify for benefits.

Five-Year Look-Back Period: To prevent abuse of the system, Medicaid has a five-year look-back period. Transfers into an irrevocable trust may incur penalties if done within this timeframe.

REVOCABLE MEDICAID TRUSTS

Revocable trusts can be altered or dissolved by the grantor at any time. However, these trusts do not provide the same level of asset protection as irrevocable trusts. Since assets in a revocable trust are considered available to the grantor, they may still be counted towards Medicaid's asset limits. Despite this limitation, revocable trusts can be beneficial for other estate planning purposes.

Be absolutely sure of the current law in your individual state regarding Medicaid qualification and disqualification. The laws vary from year to year and from state to state. Federal law may even eviscerate the Medicaid program in an attempt to cut costs for the program. *Get good advice* is the best advice when facing Medicaid qualification.

To eliminate the five-year disqualification, the application for Medicaid benefits should not be done until the disqualification period has lapsed. In the meantime, non-exempt assets can be used to pay the expenses of care and transfers of assets into an irrevocable trust will allow a Medicaid application with no worry about the lookback penalty.

Pooled trusts are a type of irrevocable trust designed for individuals with disabilities. These trusts are managed by nonprofit organizations and allow individuals to pool their resources while maintaining eligibility for public benefits. Pooled trusts offer flexibility and can provide a means to fund supplemental care and services. Special needs trusts can also play a role in Medicaid planning for individuals with disabilities. These trusts allow assets to be held for the benefit of a disabled individual without affecting their eligibility for Medicaid or Supplemental Security Income (SSI).

LEGAL CONSIDERATIONS

Navigating Medicaid trusts involves understanding various legal nuances:

State Regulations: I repeat—Medicaid programs are administered at the state level, and rules governing trusts and Medicaid qualification can vary significantly. It is crucial to consult with a local attorney specializing in elder law to ensure compliance with state regulations.

Tax Implications: Transfers to Medicaid trusts can have tax consequences. Irrevocable trusts may affect estate taxes, and income generated by trust assets can be taxable to the grantor or beneficiaries.

Trustee Selection: Choosing the right trustee is vital, as they will manage the trust assets and ensure compliance with Medicaid rules. This role can be filled by a trusted family member, friend, or a professional trustee.

Documentation and Disclosure: Proper documentation is necessary to establish the trust and its terms. Additionally, it may be necessary to disclose the existence of the trust during the Medicaid application process.

PRACTICAL APPLICATIONS OF MEDICAID TRUSTS

Long-Term Care Planning: Individuals planning for long-term care often use Medicaid trusts to protect assets while ensuring access to necessary healthcare services. By placing assets in an irrevocable trust, individuals can meet Medicaid's asset limits, allowing them to qualify for benefits without depleting their savings.

Estate Planning: Medicaid trusts can play a significant role in estate planning, allowing individuals to specify how their assets will be managed and distributed after their death. This can include designating beneficiaries and ensuring that funds are used for specific purposes, such as education or healthcare.

Caregiver Support: For individuals receiving care at home, Medicaid trusts can provide financial support to caregivers. Funds from the trust can be used to compensate family members or professionals providing care, thus enhancing the quality of life for the individual.

Transitioning to Nursing Care: When transitioning from home care to a nursing facility, Medicaid trusts can help cover costs while maintaining eligibility for benefits. The trust can ensure that sufficient funds are available for both care and quality of life enhancements.

Medicaid trusts are powerful tools for asset protection and long-term care planning. By understanding the types of trusts available, the legal implications, and their practical applications, individuals can better navigate the complexities of Medicaid eligibility. For anyone considering Medicaid planning, consulting with a knowledgeable attorney is crucial to ensure that trusts are set up correctly and in alignment with state regulations. Through effective use of Medicaid trusts, individuals can protect their assets and secure necessary care, providing peace of mind for themselves and their families.

A trust can provide some protection against Medicaid recovery, but it depends on the type of trust and how it's structured. Generally, irrevocable trusts may shield assets from Medicaid estate recovery, while revocable trusts do not, except as previously stated.

When you set up an irrevocable trust, the assets are no longer considered part of your estate, which can help protect them from being reclaimed by Medicaid after your passing. However, there are strict rules and timing considerations, such as the look-back period (typically five years), of which you need to be aware.

Consulting with an attorney who specializes in elder law or estate planning can provide tailored advice based on your specific situation.

For all estates we evaluate each situation for asset type, available techniques, family needs, and come up with the simplest plan that will put your assets into the hands of your heirs with the least possible cost in money and far fewer time delays.

CHAPTER 12

Ladybird Deeds

In *How to Avoid Probate for Everyone*, I discussed the use of trusts as a primary planning technique which, if utilized properly with careful funding, would avoid probate altogether. Some estates have as their primary asset the person's home or other real estate. In that case it is often appropriate, if allowed in your jurisdiction, to create a beneficiary deed (also called an enhanced life estate deed or ladybird deed) that would allow the owner to deed the property to their heirs either equally or in shares, while reserving to themselves the right to sell, mortgage, give away, or rent the real estate and keep all the proceeds of that transaction. Then, at the death of the property owner, all the heirs need to do is file a death certificate with the registry of the deeds where the property is located (and sometimes also requiring an affidavit regarding the transaction) and the property is at that instant owned by the named heirs.

A VALUABLE PLANNING TOOL

This method of avoiding probate using this type of deed is used more often these days since it addresses a situation where the primary asset owned is real estate. The way this works is the person who owns the property (the grantor) signs a deed transferring title to one or more other people in equal or unequal shares. However, the deed states that during the lifetime of the grantor he or she may sell the property, mortgage it, or give it away to whomever the grantor chooses without the permission of the grantee. When the grantor dies, if he or she still owns the property, the grantor's death certificate is recorded, which acts to transfer full title to the grantees. This transfer would be subject to any mortgages or other encumbrances on the title so that would have to be paid, refinanced, or the property sold. These deeds are now recognized by most states as legal although the title "ladybird deed" might not be used. It is an easy and inexpensive way of avoiding probate on the real estate. And there is no rule that limits you to one parcel of real estate. However, it is only appropriate if you do not need the asset management functions of a revocable or irrevocable trust.

Some people have multiple properties, and they could prepare ladybird deeds on each of them and even use different grantees on each. You can create a ladybird deed with some of your assets and have other assets controlled by a revocable trust. Or, if the remaining assets after deducting the value of the deeded property is below the threshold for small estate status according to state law, there may be available a short-form probate process, which would allow the administering of the estate by a short-term affidavit rather than a full-blown probate procedure.

Warning: In some states the ladybird deed and other beneficiary deeds must be recorded with the state deeds office before the death of the person making the deed. If it is not recorded by that time, then it becomes void at the time of death of the grantor and must then be probated along with any other assets still in the name of the grantor. While the record-before-death rule is only applicable in some states, the best practice is to record it before death in any state where the property is located. Laws change and the best advice is to record now and not take a chance that the law will change and disallow your deed. Also, be sure that your state allows the use of the ladybird deed.

Even in states that require recording prior to death, the recorded deed can still be revoked by the maker of the deed by recording a revocation of the deed or recording a new modified ladybird deed. All the power of the grantor to sell, mortgage, gift, or lease the property remain, even though the deed has been recorded. Grantees, that is, those who would get ownership of the property at the time of death of the grantor, do not get any additional rights to the property while the grantor is alive, and the grantor does not need their signature or permission to manage or dispose of the property during his or her lifetime. They are contingent beneficiaries—what the law might call remaindermen.

There is no requirement generally that those who are named as the beneficiaries of the ladybird deed must be treated equally. The grantor of the deed can direct that the shares of the beneficiaries be in percentages or shares totaling one hundred percent.

Here are some key points about a transfer on death deed or ladybird deed:

- **Owner's Control:** With a ladybird deed, the property owner maintains full control and ownership rights over the property during their lifetime. They can sell, mortgage, or transfer the property without obtaining consent from the beneficiaries named in the deed.
- **Transfer on Death:** The deed specifies one or more beneficiaries who will receive the property upon the owner's death. The transfer of ownership occurs automatically, bypassing the probate process, which can help simplify the transfer of assets.
- **Retained Rights:** Unlike a traditional transfer of ownership, the ladybird deed allows the property owner to retain certain rights during their lifetime. These rights typically include the ability to live in the property, collect rent, and make changes or improvements as desired.
- **Medicaid Planning:** Ladybird deeds are commonly used in Medicaid planning. By retaining a life estate in the property, the owner may avoid having the property count as an available asset for Medicaid eligibility purposes.

- **Legal Requirements:** The specific requirements for a transfer on death or ladybird deed vary by jurisdiction.

If there is more than one beneficiary, the grantor can also specify whether or not they are receiving title as joint with right of survivorship (JWROS). Married couples may elect to take ownership as tenants by the entireties or as tenants in common. This is important since with JWROS ownership, tenants by the entireties, no joint owner can transfer his or her share without the consent of the other joint owners. In a tenant in common ownership, the co-owners can sell or mortgage their share and transfer their ownership interest in their own trust or will without the permission of the co-owners.

CHAPTER 13

Gifting

Gifting is another way of passing on assets without probate. But this works only with titled assets like vehicles, watercraft, and real estate. It also has to be the right sort of joint ownership. In real estate if you want to gift an immediate ownership interest with others it should be titled as your name, then the name of the other owner, as "joint tenants with right of survivorship." So now the property belongs to the grantor and grantees equally, and at the death of one owner the others automatically own the property outright. The downside is that neither of you can sell or mortgage the property without the consent of the other, even though it was all yours before the title was changed.

REDUCE YOUR TAXABLE ESTATE, PROS AND CONS

Another form of joint ownership is called "tenants in common," in which each co-owner has an undivided percentage share in the property and that each owner can sell, devise, or gift his or her share of the asset without the consent of the others. At death, the dead person's share is subject to probate. Vehicles can also be titled that way sometimes with the acronym JWROS (joint with right of survivorship). It is also possible in some states to title a vehicle as either/or so that the title would look like this: "Robert Smith or Jim Jones." In that case either person can sell the vehicle without the consent of the other.

One issue with joint ownership is a tax problem. If you gift a share of an asset so that it becomes a joint asset, your tax basis

63

for capital gains tax purposes is the value as of the date of the transfer. Years later, if you sell your interest in an asset which has appreciated in value, you have a gain equal to the value on the date of sale minus the value on the date of the gift. For real estate this could be a huge tax hit. If instead you left the asset to be part of your inherited property, the tax basis is the value as of the date of inheritance so if the sale is made at that time there is no gain due to the stepped-up tax basis and therefore no capital gains tax.

If you give away your assets, then there would be nothing left in your name to probate. Of course, a gift is a permanent transfer of ownership, so you would have to rely on the good intentions of the recipient and hope they aren't faced with lawsuits, divorce, or bankruptcy that would negate your generous intention. There are no takebacks on gifts. Also ask your financial planner or accountant about the tax basis for capital gains on gifted property or state inheritance tax. As of this writing, only six states have a state-level inheritance tax. These states are Iowa, Kentucky, Maryland, Nebraska, New Jersey, and Pennsylvania. The tax rates are up to 16% with varying levels of exemptions. You need to look at your situation to see if gifting to reduce your taxable estate is appropriate for your situation and in your state.

But why not avoid the complexity of trusts and wills altogether by just adding the names of your heirs to your deeds? This is a simple solution to avoiding probate, but one that is fraught with potential problems and expensive unintended results.

By adding your children to the deed, you are making them co-owners of the property. This means they have legal rights to the property, and any major decision involving the home (like selling or refinancing) would require their approval. If there's any disagreement, it could complicate your ability to manage the property as you wish. Other considerations:

Gift Tax Consequences: Transferring ownership by adding your child's name may be considered a gift, potentially triggering gift taxes. If the value of the property exceeds the annual gift tax exemption limit (as set by the IRS), you may have to file a gift tax return and could be liable for taxes.

Medicaid Eligibility and Estate Recovery: Adding your children's names to your deed might interfere with Medicaid eligibility. If you apply for Medicaid within five years of transferring the property, this could count as a "transfer for less than fair market value," resulting in a penalty period where you are ineligible for Medicaid.

After your death, Medicaid can also recover assets, and transferring property may not protect it from being included in Medicaid estate recovery. Be aware, though, that Medicaid eligibility is controlled by the state law of your residence and varies by jurisdiction.

Loss of Flexibility: Once your children's names are on the deed, any decisions to sell, mortgage, or transfer the property become more complex. Your children would need to agree to the transaction, and you could lose flexibility in managing the property for your own needs, including any financial decisions related to it.

Instead of adding your children's names to your deed, consider alternative estate planning tools, such as living trusts, transfer-on-death deeds, or wills. These options provide more control and protection from taxes and legal complications without immediately transferring ownership.

CHAPTER 14

Estate Planning Using Beneficiary Designations

Most investment assets can be transferred at death by using beneficiary designations. When we say beneficiary, most folks will assume we are talking about life insurance, but other accounts can utilize beneficiary designations. This is true for bank and credit union checking and savings accounts (though your bank clerk might not have mentioned that to you when you opened the account), CDs, money markets, brokerage accounts, tax-deferred accounts, and others. So beneficiary designations are not just for life insurance policies.

If you have created a trust, the beneficiary of the account can be the trust. That would allow the trust distribution plan to control the distribution to the heirs named in the trust. If you are married, you could name your spouse as primary beneficiary and the trust as the alternate beneficiary. Or you could leave an asset to a person who is not an heir named in the trust so that person would not be subject to any restrictions that may have been required by the trust distribution plan.

Beware of changing the ownership of deferred income accounts such as IRAs. Changing the ownership could result in immediate taxation of the deferred income. What you want to do is make your spouse the primary beneficiary of the deferred income in order to preserve any roll-over options that might be available. The alternate beneficiary could be your children or one or more of your other heirs. If you have a trust, it could be

67

a primary or alternate beneficiary, subject to tax rules. The rules, regulations, and options regarding beneficiary designation of tax-deferred accounts change frequently, so it is imperative that you consult your financial planner or the plan administrator for current rules.

You do not have to treat all beneficiaries equally. You could divide the death benefit into percentages or shares. It is sometimes allowed to place conditions on the percentage-based designation, for example, attaining a certain age. If you have a trust, you could assign that share to the trustee of the trust and the trust conditions could manage the funds until the conditions are met.

CHAPTER 15

Should You Write Your Own Will or Trust?

Should you write your own will? Lawyers are expensive. The upside of having a lawyer prepare your will is that you can be confident that it was done correctly. On the other hand, there are will forms available for free online which claim that the fill-in-the-blank forms were originally prepared by a lawyer and are perfectly legal in every state. I searched the internet by using the keywords "make your own will free" and got 4,620,000 results. So, it is pretty easy to make your own will. But is using a free template form right for you? And is it legally sufficient in your state? There is no one-size-fits-all for wills and most other legal documents.

DOWNLOAD AT YOUR PERIL

First, you have to realize that while the rules are similar in each state as to creating a valid will, they are not exactly the same. Basic rules have to be included as to witnessing and signing requirements, identification of heirs, and even notarization. The will maker must have so-called testamentary capacity. That is, he or she must have an understanding as to assets they own, who are their objects of affection, i.e., family relationships, and that the document they are signing is indeed a will. Witnesses help verify those requirements. The will may also name the people who are to be the executors (also called personal representatives) to carry out the terms of the will.

69

70   Beneficiary Guide for Everyone

The first question to be answered is whether you need a will at all. If you have no will and die, a will can set out in writing your wishes as to the distribution of your probatable assets existing at the time of your death. But very often what your will instructs is exactly what the state statutes would do if you died without a will. For example, I often begin a client interview by asking what the clients want done with their estate after their death. I might be told that the couple want each other to inherit from them and after they are both gone, then their adult children would equally divide the remaining assets. I then tell them they do not need a will to accomplish that result since that is exactly what the state law would dictate without a will. And the probate process in most cases is the same whether there is a will or not. They need to understand the value of a revocable trust in avoiding probate and managing assets left to heirs.

So, the creation of a will or trust is best handled by an experienced estate attorney. But what about handling the details of the trust settlement and distribution of trust assets to heirs? Can you settle the estate without a lawyer being involved? Settling a non-probate trust-based estate can vary depending on the specific circumstances and the laws of your jurisdiction. While it is possible to handle the process yourself, it is sometimes recommended to seek the assistance of an attorney if the estate is complex or substantial. Having said that, many of the duties of the trustee in wrapping up all the estate issues are more clerical than legal.

Here are a few reasons why you might consider consulting with a lawyer:

- **Understanding Legal Requirements:** An attorney can help you navigate the legal requirements and obligations associated with settling a trust-based estate. They can provide guidance on the specific laws in your jurisdiction and ensure that you fulfill all necessary obligations.

Should You Write Your Own Will or Trust? 71

- **Document Preparation:** Trust administration often involves preparing legal documents, such as notifications to beneficiaries, creditors, and government agencies. An attorney can help you draft and review these documents to ensure they are legally sound and accurately reflect your intentions.
- **Tax Considerations:** Depending on the size of the estate and the applicable tax laws, there may be tax implications to consider. An attorney with expertise in estate planning and tax matters can provide advice on minimizing tax liabilities and guide you through the required filings.
- **Resolving Disputes:** In some cases, disagreements or conflicts may arise among beneficiaries or other interested parties. An attorney can assist in mediating or resolving these disputes to help ensure a smooth administration process.
- **Peace of Mind:** Engaging an attorney can provide you with peace of mind, knowing that a legal professional is overseeing the settlement process. This can alleviate stress and minimize the risk of errors or oversights that could have legal consequences down the line.

While it may be tempting to handle the process yourself to save on legal fees, the complexity of trust administration and potential legal implications make it advisable to consult with an attorney. They can guide you through the process, help you avoid potential pitfalls, and ensure that the estate is settled in accordance with applicable laws. However, you should offer to do the non-legal work yourself. There is no good reason to pay hundreds of dollars per hour for what amounts to clerical work, such as filing claims for beneficiary payouts, dealing with realtors to sell a house, and securing a tax ID for the trust, among other things.

A common fringe benefit offered by employers nowadays is prepaid legal services. These provide full coverage in most cases for preparation of a trust, will, power of attorney, and medical directives. Check with your employee benefits people to see if you can enroll and find out what is covered.

Sometimes even very large estates can be handled in a simplified manner, avoiding probate altogether. There could be the house with no mortgage and various investments that can be left to heirs through beneficiary designations. If we put the house into ladybird deed, also called a beneficiary deed or transfer on death deed, there would be no assets left out that would need to be probated and not require complex probate procedures.

But what if there is a mortgage on the inherited property? If you inherit a real estate property, such as a house, that has an existing mortgage, there are a few important factors to consider and an attorney can often provide guidance. Here's some information that may help you understand the situation:

- **Contact the Lender:** As the new owner, you should notify the mortgage lender about the situation. They will provide guidance on how to proceed and what steps to take. Ask about any documentation or legal requirements they may have.
- **Review the Mortgage Terms:** Familiarize yourself with the terms and conditions of the existing mortgage. Take note of the interest rate, repayment schedule, outstanding balance, and any other relevant details. Understanding the terms will help you make informed decisions.
- **Determine Your Options:** Generally, you have a few options when inheriting a property with a mortgage:
  - **Assume the mortgage:** In some cases, the lender may allow you to assume the mortgage. This means you agree to take over the existing mortgage under the same terms and conditions. However, the lender will likely assess your financial situation and creditworthiness before approving the assumption.

Should You Write Your Own Will or Trust?   73

- **Refinance the mortgage:** If assuming the mortgage isn't an option or you want to explore alternatives, you can consider refinancing the loan. Refinancing involves applying for a new mortgage to pay off the existing one. This allows you to negotiate new terms and potentially lower interest rates.
- **Pay off the mortgage:** If you have sufficient funds or assets available, you can choose to pay off the mortgage in full. This relieves you of the ongoing mortgage payments and gives you full ownership of the property.
- **Seek Professional Advice:** Dealing with inherited property and mortgages can be complex. It's advisable to consult with professionals such as estate attorneys, financial advisors, or mortgage brokers. They can provide personalized guidance based on your specific situation and help you make informed decisions.

Remember, the process may vary depending on your location, the specific mortgage agreement, and other factors. It's crucial to gather all relevant information and seek professional advice to navigate the situation effectively.

Of course, there are other considerations in estate settlement. If there are minor children, the naming of a guardian would be in order. Minor guardianships do not have to be in a will since a guardian can be appointed via a standalone document. Regardless of how you do it, it is a very good idea to include the guardianship choice in your will; if a proper guardian is not named, then someone else will be appointed who might not be your first choice. Courts normally give preference to the parents' choice unless someone objects and can prove that the guardianship choice is improper.

What if you have disabled heirs? Sometimes it is a bad idea to leave money equally to your children. They might be disabled and receiving need-based benefits such as Medicaid. If you leave such a disabled beneficiary an inheritance, it may be

74   **Beneficiary Guide for Everyone**

that the state would take away those benefits and require that the inherited money be used for the care of the heir. When the money is used up to the point where they again qualify for the aid, the heir would have to reapply for the benefits. To protect the disabled person, we can direct in a will or trust that the share of that person be held in trust until the person's death but can in the meantime use those funds for his or her benefit in amounts and for purposes that would not disqualify them.

Or there might be a child that you want to leave out of the will. You can certainly disinherit anyone you like and leave your money to whomever you want. But if you do not include the name of the disinherited child, the presumption of the court by statute might be that you forgot to mention them and that it was an error in the will, so the disinherited child would be able to take a share regardless of your actual intention. So, you would need to not only say that the disinheritance was intentional, but also that anyone in general who is not mentioned is not to be considered an heir. That keeps at bay the purported heir who claims to be an illegitimate child of the will maker.

Another thing that can be included is a no-contest clause that says that if someone successfully contests the will, their share will be reduced to one dollar and their expectancy cannot be assigned. That language discourages will contests since even if they win, they lose, bearing in mind that they would have to pay their attorneys for the will contest.

While the reasons named above can be put into a will, the question remains, do you really need a will?

When interviewing clients, I explain that I see my role as their attorney to set up a plan that allows their wishes to be followed with the least trouble, time, and expense to their children. They always agree that is also their goal.

That goal is not achieved by having a will.

Wills have to be probated, trusts do not.

Should You Write Your Own Will or Trust? 75

All of the situations described above that call for careful planning can be put into the language of a trust. The trust can then be administered by the successor trustee with no court intervention and no attorney involvement with no set deadlines, delays, and in most cases no taxes or court costs.

CHAPTER 16

How to Guarantee that Your Estate Is Probated

We make trusts for two primary reasons. First, to be sure that your assets are distributed to the people you have named and under the conditions you set forth. Second, to avoid the time and expense of the probate process. Both of those goals can be thwarted by improper planning.

EVEN WITH A TRUST

A not uncommon problem is the failure to properly set out to whom your estate is to be distributed and under what conditions. For example, a trust may say that persons A, B, and C are to divide the assets remaining in the trust at your death. If one of them dies before you, their share is to go to his or her children, and if there are no surviving children, then that share goes to the other two surviving heirs. Time passes and the grantor decides that he will change the trust by an amendment to require that all heirs must be members of the grantor's church, or their share will lapse. He does this without a lawyer by crossing off and initialing the original instructions and writing the new requirements in the margin of the document. He made no provision to cover a likely situation where none of the heirs agreed to join the church.

Obviously, there are problems with this fact situation. The likely result will be the presumptive heirs putting this in the lap of a probate judge. The judge could rule in several ways.

She might uphold the conditions but since the plan failed, could treat the trust as an intestate estate, leaving all the assets to the heirs at law—so A, B, and C would inherit after the estate is probated. Or she could ignore the handwritten and unwitnessed changes and allow the trust to continue, settling the estate through the guidance of the named trustee in the trust. Alternatively, she could uphold the changes and direct the estate to escheat the assets to the state since no beneficiaries met the conditions set out in the amended trust.

Avoiding probate also avoids the problem of a probate judge interpreting your directions in a way that you might not have intended.

The lessons here? Don't do your own legal work, and be sure to have a written plan that covers all contingencies. A simple statement that you want your entire estate to go to the first of your grandchildren to become a dentist is not a good plan unless you then say what happens to the estate if none of your grandchildren ever qualify.

Then there are trusts that are unfunded. At the time the trust was created, the clients and their attorney make sure that all the assets owned by the grantor are either put into the name of the trust or have beneficiaries named who would inherit outside the trust. It is common, however, to find that at the time of death many assets were not directed either to a beneficiary or to the trust. So, we get probate to straighten out the unfunded trust.

Having an improperly drawn trust is one way to get into probate court. Another is failing to resolve disputes over the trust settlement process. We pay judges to solve disputes over such things as asset valuations, distribution of personal property items, determining the competency of the deceased at the time the documents were created, whether there was undue influence over a person when they made their estate plan, and other disputes, including all issues related to the trustees' fees and expenses including alleged fraud. All of these issues can be avoided if the estate plan is properly drafted. This means you stay out of probate court and maintain family harmony.

Question: My brother hated me, and we had not spoken for years after I took my mother's side in a very contentious divorce proceeding. My brother died recently, and I was surprised that I was included in his will. The thing is that he left me some real estate that had once contained a gas station, now boarded up. I have found out that he was probably not doing me any favors with this so-called gift. The underground tanks are in line to be replaced since they leaked and contaminated the ground and likely the groundwater. The property is consequently not saleable, and the owners are legally on the hook for environmental cleanup. I don't know how much that will cost but I suspect it will be a lot. What do I do since there is no way I can pay for this?

Answer: Let's hope that your brother did not have evil intentions by giving you this white elephant. The good news is that you are not required to accept this inherited property. You should see a lawyer or whoever is handling the estate to prepare the appropriate paperwork for you to disclaim this inheritance. It would be a good idea also to have your attorney check to see if there are governmental funds available to pay for the cleanup. The so-called Brownfield laws might allow for grants to clean up environmentally damaged sites. If so, the joke could be on your brother, and you might end up with a saleable property.

Family Conflict Resolution. Stop the fighting. When a family member dies, the initial reaction is to bring the family together in shared grief. But that reaction doesn't always last and can vary, with some family relationships more likely than others to have issues with each other. The makeup of your family and extended family can lead to understandable conflict.

For example, the traditional family, consisting of father, mother, and children may be less likely to experience intra-family conflict than a blended family situation where there are stepchildren and ex-spouses to consider. Sometimes the parental units have differing ideas as to how the assets should be distributed or preserved.

If the documents, such as trusts, wills, and beneficiary designations are carefully prepared, so as to be bulletproof, there will be less chance of a successful court challenge. The deceased person's decisions can still be challenged but not on the basis of what is or is not fair.

CHAPTER 17

Will Contests

After a decedent's death it is normally impossible to change the directions of the decedent as to how much is left to the heirs and the conditions that might be attached to their bequests, but there are situations where the designations themselves can be contested. The will or beneficiary designations could be found to be fraudulent or defective to the extent that the beneficiary could lose their share. We also talk about the responsibilities of the estate executor in managing assets, paying debts, and continuing supervision of bequests over time if required in the original documents. Sometimes we ask the court to claw back assets that were transferred improperly to caretakers or others who would not be considered an heir.

CONTESTING A WILL OR TRUST: GROUNDS FOR OBJECTION

The rights of beneficiaries allow competing heirs to use the courts to challenge the decisions made by a decedent. Court challenges to beneficiary designations are rare, unlike challenges to a trust, or even less likely to a will. The rights of a beneficiary are spelled out in the following pages by examples from my law practice. I will also show beneficiary-based plans that can be used in even modest estates to minimize misunderstandings, family disharmony, and estrangement.

A will contest is not a competition between competing wills, although it could be. The purpose of probate historically is a court confirming a person's will as being valid due to proper language, by a person who is of age of majority or legally emancipated, mentally competent, properly executed, with a signature and signed in front of two witnesses. As with most things legal, there are exceptions to these requirements. For example, a handwritten holographic will.

It must be in writing. Writing does not just mean printed or typed. Handwritten wills can be perfectly legal if they conform to state statutes. These rules vary from state to state, but generally: it must be written entirely in the handwriting of the maker, state that it is intended as a will, be dated, and signed. Witnessing is not usually a requirement.

These "holographic wills" are often challenged. There are exceptions to the signature requirement if a person due to physical disability is unable to sign. Another person can then sign for him. Notarization is not a requirement, although having a will notarized can make its admission to probate easier. There is also a way of witnessing and notarization of a will called a self-proving clause that eliminates the need to have witnesses testify in court as to the state of mind and fitness, of a testator.

Sometimes people call the process breaking the will. The decision to try to get a will disqualified is made for several reasons, mostly financial. It might be that someone who thought they were going to be included in the final distribution of the estate assets was left out or given a smaller share than they expected. Or it could be that the directives in the will, though legally enforceable, were just considered unfair by an affected person. It is natural for children of the decedent to assume that they should all be treated equally, though that is not a legal requirement in a will. And what is fair for blended families with stepbrothers, stepsisters, stepmothers, or stepfathers? What seems fair to the ones included as beneficiaries likely won't be automatically approved by the ones left out.

The law recognizes and directs who would be an heir if there was no will. In such cases, the laws of intestacy lay out who inherits, typically following marital and bloodline relationships.

Will Contests
83

So those not in the will but who would be in the intestacy line of inheritance have strong motives to overturn the will and not let it be admitted to probate. With no will, the will's directions as to who inherits, when they inherit, how much they inherit, and who is in charge of the estate (the executor, administrator, or personal representative) will be ignored and a previous will should be admitted to probate. If there was none, then the state law would have to be followed and the intestate heirs would inherit.

Most states recognize several reasons why a will should be considered invalid.

1. **Lack of proper drafting or execution.** There are specific procedures for the drafting and signing of a will that must be proven to have been followed to make the will valid. It must be signed by the person making the will who has had their signature witnessed, typically by two witnesses, who attest that they knew who the person was and that they knew they were making a will. While the general rule is that a will, to be valid, must have two disinterested witnesses who sign, attesting to having seen the person sign the will and that they appeared to know what they were doing, there is an exception for so-called holographic or handwritten wills. If you want to make a challenge to a will less likely, you can add a self-proving clause and notarization. The self-proving clause eliminates the need for will witnesses to come into court to testify as to the will's execution. The legal presumption is that the will was properly executed.

2. **Lack of testamentary capacity.** Okay, the meaning of that is not self-evident. What it means is the person who is making the will has to understand first that they are making a will, and second, that they understand and remember their family relationships. Sometimes it is phrased as understanding the objects of their affection or bounty. Someone who does not remember the

names of their children or that they actually have children probably does not have the mental ability to make a reasoned decision on who would be their heirs. Or it might be that they can't identify the assets that they own or what they are worth.

3. **Coercion or undue influence.** A common reason for contesting a will is that the person making the will was either coerced or unduly influenced to make the will. Perhaps a caretaker ingratiated himself to the testator and convinced him to make a will that benefitted the caretaker and excluded the person's natural heirs. The convincing could have been coercion or fear. The caretaker may have threatened to abandon the testator unless the desired will was prepared. The will must have been done as the intentional act of the person and not at the direction of someone else.

4. **Fraud.** Fraud is another reason for contesting a will. It may have been forged and we might need to rely on handwriting analysis or witness testimony to establish its authenticity. Sometimes a will is destroyed by a person who had been disinherited. If a will is lost or destroyed and it cannot be proven to have existed, a prior will could be presented to the court as the will of the deceased even though it was supposedly revoked by the language of the will that was destroyed. The reason we have judges in probate is to listen to evidence as to what is the proper legal will of the deceased and admit that one to probate, even if the actual document cannot be found. It is a good idea to file your will with the court to hold it for safekeeping until your death in order to avoid illegal shenanigans.

While not strictly a will contest, portions of a will can be contested. For example, the named executor (a.k.a. personal representative) might not be a suitable person to act as executor of the will. Other relatives or heirs could ask the court to appoint

Will Contests

a different person to be executor. Reasons and proof would be presented in court and the judge could decide who the executor should be. If the named executor has a history of mismanaging the assets of the deceased, or might have other issues such as substance abuse or is a convicted felon, that would be taken into consideration.

Challenges to a will are sometimes made without much evidence in order to delay the proceedings and perhaps extort a settlement payoff to the person making the challenge. As a practical matter contested probate can take months or even years to resolve. Paying someone off might be the least costly way to resolve the estate even if doing so creates bad feelings in the family.

A no-contest clause in the will can help avoid will contests. This is a statement to the effect that if someone contests the will and succeeds, the maximum amount they can receive through the will is one dollar. This discourages most potential challenges—especially since the person making the challenge will also have to pay their own attorney fees to make the challenge. There may also be an arbitration clause in which the contesting parties would have to participate.

Before considering filing to contest a will, remember that there is a limited time frame to make the contest. The time when you can file will vary, depending upon in what state the probate case is filed, but it is typically about six months from the time the case was filed. Also, remember that litigation is very expensive, consisting mostly of attorney fees. Most lawyers will not take on a case on a contingency basis. Even at the typical one-third of the recovery, one-third of nothing is nothing. Expect to pay by the hour and that there are going to be many hours.

A trust can also be challenged the same as if were a will, even if it is a probate-avoiding type trust. Normally a trust-based estate is designed to be settled without court intervention, thereby saving the time and expense of probate court supervision. However, an interested party, such as an omitted heir, can file for probate and seek court supervision of the trust settlement, and even ask that the trustee named in the trust document be replaced with another person. Sometimes that person will be a court-appointed estate administrator who is typically an attorney. The trust can even be invalidated by the court based on one or more of the will contest objections named above.

We typically insert in the trust document the clause about limiting the amount inherited by a successful will contestant, but if the trust is invalidated, then that clause means nothing.

Oral trusts are allowed in many states. That would be, for example, where oral promises were made to an heir as to an expected inheritance. We need witnesses who have firsthand knowledge of the promise and that can be upheld in court even without a written document. Maybe something like a parent promising to leave the family farm to a child who relies on the farm for his livelihood, even though there were other children who would otherwise be in line to inherit.

Question: My mom and dad retired to the Orlando area from Michigan a few years ago. Mom died and Dad now lives alone in their mobile home. My brother and I live about 1,200 miles away, so we can't see him very often. He won't talk about moving north to be near us. I think he has, or is getting, dementia based on my telephone calls with him. When I ask him questions about how he's doing, he tells me that Doris is taking care of him. I finally got to talk to Doris and found out she is a neighbor who has been helping him with paying his bills, some cooking, and taking him to his doctor appointments since he can no longer drive. I can't get any information from Doris on his finances. I talked to the branch manager of his bank and was told Doris was an authorized signer on his accounts. Doris says that's not my business and guilts me by saying someone has to take care of him since I am not. I fear she is draining his resources and will disappear when the money's gone. He has a will with my brother and me listed as heirs, but who knows whether he might have made out another one leaving everything to Doris.

Answer: On the one hand it's great that there is someone to take care of him day-to-day. On the other hand, you are right to be concerned about her taking over his personal and financial affairs. The best thing is to take a bit of time to go to Florida, talk to him privately, and find out as much as you can about where things stand with his mental capacity and what has been happening with his money. If you can't take him back home with you, it would be a good idea to talk to a Florida attorney and/or the local Adult Protective Services to see about appointing someone, preferably you or your brother, as his adult guardian and conservator. Doris could be kept on as a paid caretaker if she likes.

The court also has the authority to make her account for his funds and order a return of any monies she may have misappropriated if there was some wrongdoing. His will won't do you much good if all his assets have been used up during his lifetime.

Question: What do I do about my mother's debts? We had no idea she had so many credit cards and most of them are either maxed out or almost so. One creditor wants us to enter into a repayment agreement and alternatively has offered to take half of what's owed as full payment.

Answer: It is not unusual for a parent to die with debt. Sometimes after the death of one partner the other faces a major decline in income. This can happen because of two things. First is that the Social Security of the first spouse to die ends. In fact, the Social Security administration will demand that the last check be returned, since benefits are considered as paid in advance. So while the survivor gets to choose to take either his or her own

(Continued . . .)

Social Security or, if it is larger, the amount that was being paid to the partner, the income still drops.

The second reason is because of how pensions may end with the death of the recipient. In some plans there is a choice allowed to instruct as to when benefits start. The recipient can take a larger monthly benefit for life, or take a smaller benefit that continues for the lifetime of the surviving spouse. Certain annuities can have the same provisions. Without other resources the survivor may end up relying on credit cards to maintain a normal lifestyle for as long as possible.

The heirs do not have to pay for the credit cards of the deceased unless the heirs are co-owners of the card account or if the deceased was a resident of a community property state. An heir can even be an authorized signer without being a co-owner and still does not have to pay the account. Collection agencies often try to get the survivors to pay even though they have no legal obligation to pay. What you should do is send photocopies of the death certificate to the credit card company along with the cards themselves, which should be cut in half, and a note saying the account should be closed. Do not use the cards again, even if you are only an authorized signer, or you may revive the debt and must pay it yourself.

The card company might still be paid if there is a probate estate opened, since all known creditors must be notified of the probate, and they can file a claim for payment with the probate court. If there are sufficient assets they will be paid in full or if, after payment of family allowances, expenses of administration, taxes, court costs, and fees there is not enough to pay in full, they may get a percentage of the debt paid to them.

Understand the grounds for contesting a will or other document involved in a decedent's estate. In the end it is mostly about money. Those who complain about the will or trust are the ones who believe they were somehow shortchanged by the decedent. However, they also say there are very clear reasons

Will Contests 89

why a will or a trust or even a beneficiary designation should be reversed. If they win, then the estate will likely be considered intestate and so be subject to the full probate proceeding as well as using the formula in the state law as to who are the heirs.

Okay, Uncle Fred made out his will and left everything to his next-door neighbor, whom we will call Bob, not you. Uncle Fred never married and had no children. Since your parents are deceased and you had no siblings nor any other aunts or uncles, you assumed you, being your uncle's closest blood relative blood relative, would be the one who inherited. Not a big problem since Uncle Fred only had his house and a ten-year-old car, but still . . . Then there was the fact that Uncle Fred was a bit off, mentally. He didn't recognize you when you stopped for a visit and talked about your father—his brother—as if he were still alive. He was also convinced that he owned a farm in Guatemala with 100 hectares of land and said he was giving that to your dad, whom he knew liked to farm. So, Uncle Fred was not all there, which was clear if you spent more than a half-hour with him.

To get some help handling the apparently incompetent Uncle Fred, most people go to an attorney they know or who is referred by family and friends. The lawyer might start talking about "testamentary capacity"—a new term to you. If Uncle Fred did not recognize his so-called objects of affection, that is, the existence or acknowledgment of his family relationships, then this is one of the factors a judge might use to determine his competence. Bob knew nothing about the will and was surprised he was named as heir since he and Uncle Fred had only a mailbox-nod sort of relationship.

Whenever someone comes to me for estate services, I have to be assured that the person seeking the will or trust knows who I am and why he is there. I will ask the person who brought him to step outside while I talk to the client alone. Most of the time they know exactly why they came to see me. I have, however, had cases where the client says they don't know who the person is who brought them to me. I would not do any sort of

90   **Beneficiary Guide for Everyone**

will or trust for the client. My suspicion is that the caretaker is attorney shopping and ultimately will find one who will do the will regardless of the client's observable mental incapacity.

I find it helpful if we take video of the interview in the event litigation should occur. Video can often clearly show a person's lack of cognitive dissonance, symptoms of dementia, or that the person knows exactly what she is doing and can respond to questions regarding her family relationships and financial situation.

THE PROCESS OF PROVING A WILL

Through investigation or discovery, trying to prove a will as valid or not requires similar steps.

1. Examine the will in question and any related documents. This includes:
   - The original will and any copies.
   - Correspondence or notes related to the creation of the will. Does the will contain a no-contest provision?
   - Previous wills or codicils (amendments to the will).
2. Gather evidence. Collect evidence to support your claim. This may include:
   - Medical records or expert testimony to demonstrate lack of capacity.
   - Witnesses or evidence of undue influence or coercion.
   - Proof of fraud or improper conduct.
3. Consult with an attorney. An attorney specializing in estate law or probate matters can provide legal advice and guide you through the process. They can help:
   - Assess the strength of your case.
   - Prepare legal documents and filings.
   - Represent you in court if necessary.
4. Your attorney then files a petition or complaint with the court. If you decide to move forward, you'll need to file a petition to contest the will. This petition should be filed

Will Contests 91

in the probate court where the will is being probated. The petition must outline your reasons for contesting the will and any evidence you have.

5. Participate in the legal process. The legal process will involve:
   - Discovery: Gathering and exchanging evidence with other parties.
   - Hearings: Attending court hearings where evidence and arguments are presented.
   - Settlement negotiations: Exploring the possibility of settling the dispute out of court. Sometimes contesting a will or trust is pursued strictly for forcing a settlement. The estate might decide that paying off the challenger would be cheaper and quicker than a vigorous defense. Sounds like extortion, and it sometimes really is.

6. Consider mediation. In some cases, mediation can be an effective way to resolve disputes without going to trial. A mediator can help negotiate a settlement that is acceptable to all parties involved. The purpose is to make all parties equally unhappy with the results. In many cases the trust document will require mediation and may have a penalty provision if a person wrongfully contests the will or trust. Maybe the challenge will win but the victory may be limited to a one-dollar award as specified in the disputed document.

7. Understand the timeline and costs. The timeline and costs of contesting a will can vary widely depending on the complexity of the case, the court's schedule, and other factors. Be prepared for potentially lengthy legal proceedings and associated costs. Contesting a will is not the kind of case an attorney takes on a percentage basis. Be prepared to pay a substantial retainer.

8. Be prepared for emotional impact. Contesting a will can be emotionally taxing, especially if it involves family dynamics or close relationships. It's important

to consider the personal impact and potential strain on relationships. Families can become permanently estranged by open conflict in court proceedings with multiple attorneys involved and that would wear down all of us. In the end it's all about money. Is it worth it or is a settlement preferable?

9. Follow the court's decision. If the court decides in your favor, the will may be invalidated or modified as per the ruling. If the court rules against you, you might have the option to appeal, depending on the circumstances and legal advice.

Contesting a will is a serious matter with significant legal and personal implications. Careful consideration and professional guidance are crucial throughout this process.

WILLS FOR MILITARY PERSONNEL.

While the requirements for valid will making if you are on active duty are similar to state law requirements, they are not as stringent. A military will can be oral or written. Witness requirements can be one or none, and the serviceperson making the will does not have to be eighteen years old. Also, real estate is not generally allowed to be part of the distributable estate under the relaxed federal rules.

While most wills must be witnessed, the law sometimes allows and will validate a signed but unwitnessed will. Unlike most rules that rely on state law, the rules for the military are spelled out in federal statutes.

CHAPTER 18

Legal Rights of Beneficiaries: Knowledge Is Power

The rights of beneficiaries can vary depending on the type of trust, estate, or legal arrangement involved. However, there are some common rights that beneficiaries typically have across most situations:

Right to Information: Once a beneficiary's interest in an asset is vested, that is, at the time of death of the grantor, the beneficiary generally has the right to receive information about the trust or estate, including its terms, assets, and how they are being managed.

Right to an Accounting: Beneficiaries are usually entitled to a detailed accounting of the trust or estate's financial activities. This includes information on income, expenses, and distributions.

Right to Fair Treatment: Beneficiaries should be treated fairly and in accordance with the terms of the trust or will. Trustees and executors are required to act as fiduciaries in the best interests of the beneficiaries.

Right to Distributions: Beneficiaries have the right to receive their share of the trust or estate as outlined in the trust document or will. This can include distributions of income or principal.

Right to Challenge: Beneficiaries may have the right to challenge the actions of the trustee or executor if they believe there has been a breach of fiduciary duty or mismanagement of the trust or estate.

Right to Privacy: Beneficiaries often have the right to privacy regarding their personal information and the terms of the trust or will, though this can be subject to disclosure laws.

Right to Seek Legal Advice: Beneficiaries have the right to consult with an attorney to understand their rights and the terms of the trust or estate.

The specifics of these rights can be influenced by state laws and the terms set forth in the trust or will, so it's often a good idea for beneficiaries to consult with a legal professional for guidance tailored to their particular situation.

Question: My wife has two children from a former marriage and we had one together. If my wife dies before me, can I leave her kids out of my will or trust?"

Answer: Like most questions directed to an attorney the answer is: It depends. It depends upon the language of the will or trust or if there was neither a will nor a trust. If there was a trust, the language of the document could and often does address the issue of the rights of a surviving grantor in a joint trust to modify or revoke the trust language. In a simple case of a husband, wife, and their joint children, we often leave the surviving spouse the right to amend the trust as she or he wishes, relying on the intention of a surviving parent to take care of the children. But sometimes a fail-safe provision is added that says the right to amend or revoke the trust does not extend to disinheriting one or more of their joint children.

There are ways around that direction, however. A surviving grantor could create a new trust with a new spouse and fund it with other assets, such as a life insurance policy. That would allow the survivor to provide for a new spouse and possibly newly born children without affecting the inheritance of the first set of children.

As to a will, it is possible to disinherit children provided you make it clear that the omission of that child was intentional and not an error. Spouses, however, are not so easily disinherited. So, if the wife dies first, you can certainly leave out her children from your will since they are not your biological children. If you die first your wife would have a claim against your estate for a forced share, the amount of which depends on the law of the state of your residence at death. She could then include her children as well as yours at least to the extent of the amount of her assets at death.

If there was no will or trust, state law would determine who inherits, but those statutes normally, with some exceptions, include only the spouse and the person's legal children, born or adopted.

A will is a legal document that is in effect just written instructions to the probate court as to who gets your assets, when they get them, and who is in charge of seeing that your debts are paid and the remainder distributed to your named heirs.

While in most cases probate court should be avoided, there are some situations where the probate judge can be very helpful. There are various levels of a court's involvement with a will. Supervised probate is the most complex and time-consuming. In a supervised probate the judge may have to review and ratify nearly all actions of the named executor of the estate. Their first involvement would be to confirm the validity of the will itself. Was it properly written, witnessed, and executed? Have all the so-called interested parties been identified and notified of the proceedings? Has anyone objected to or contested to the validity of the will? There are many procedural rules that must be filed in a supervised administration. The court would ultimately agree to finalize the case after all expenses and taxes have been paid. There would be lots of attorney time involved that would require the approval of the court as far as reviewing an itemized listing of every minute spent on the case at hundreds of dollars per hour.

THE DOCUMENTS

What if the will and trust documents cannot be found? Sometimes people actually lose the will or trust or both. Sometimes wills are destroyed either accidentally or intentionally by, for example, a disinherited heir.

First, check with the local probate court to see if a copy or the original is on file. Even trusts can be registered. Failing that, try to contact the attorney who drafted it. There are lawyers who keep the original documents for "safekeeping." I suspect that sometimes the lawyer is looking forward to being the attorney for the estate. But there are procedures and laws that allow for the validation of a copy if the original cannot be found. These allow testimony from those who spoke to the decedent as to the contents of the will or trust and even the testimony, by affidavit or in person, to get the judge to probate the lost will or determine what they call the decedent's testamentary intent. Oral wills are now legal in many states and holographic wills, handwritten but not witnessed, have been provable in most states for many years.

Question: My grandfather and I were very close, and a year before his death he showed me what he said was his will. I didn't read it, but he said I would be splitting his assets with my mother, who is an only child. He was not married when he died. When I thought I could ask mom gently about the will she said she had never heard about it and that Grandpa's lawyer was taking care of probate. She said I would get nothing, but she would make sure her will left everything to me. The problem is she is married to my stepfather and I think he is planning on being first in line when mom dies. I know my grandfather had the will in his desk drawer, but when I managed to look there, I couldn't find anything. What can I do?

Answer: There are several issues here. First is determining who are the legal heirs of your grandfather if he dies without a will.

In your state, the laws of descent and distribution say that your mother would be his one and only heir. If she had died before your grandfather, then you would have been his heir. I think you need to try a few things to locate the will if it exists. It's possible that he destroyed it, or hid it somewhere else, or that your mother found it and is keeping it hidden. It is a crime to withhold or destroy someone else's will after their death. You might check with other attorneys in the area to see if he had made a new will or if a lawyer was holding it for safekeeping and is unaware of his death. People sometimes make multiple wills and the most recent one is the one that would be valid.

Discreetly discussing this with mom and mentioning that maybe someone else found it (like your stepfather, for instance) might motivate her to help you in the search or possibly miraculously "find" it. It is also possible that the estate attorney is already trying to have the lost will ratified or that he is proceeding with the will not mentioned so that it would be handled as an intestate case. (The law requires that a person in possession of the will of a deceased person turn it over to the local probate court. It would be totally unethical for the attorney to withhold it.)

Good luck and you should hope your mother puts her own affairs in order to protect you down the road. A trust would have been a far better option for her and for your grandfather.

In most states it is perfectly legal to handle the probate process yourself if you are the named executor or an heir of the deceased. Judges would prefer, though, that you be legally represented just to make the process smoother. Non-attorneys have to be schooled about the process and are not trained to deal with the rules of evidence and litigation. We do not recommend self-representation. A supervised probate can become an adversary proceeding requiring legal expertise and courtroom experience. Most heirs are going to be out of their element and may end up with more time and money involved than if they had hired an attorney to begin with.

CHAPTER 19

Estate Planning from the Heart: Distributing a Legacy in a Heartfelt Way

Thoughtful estate planning takes into account how to benefit your loved ones using beneficiary designations, wills, and trusts to avoid family conflicts while being aware of the feelings suffered by the family and heirs of the deceased.

Navigating Family: Dealing with the death of a loved one is an emotionally challenging experience that can be accompanied by a range of issues. These can manifest in behavioral changes that can cause disruption in family relationships and even estrangement that can last for years. It is important, therefore, to understand the types of grief that can be experienced so that a level of understanding is possible when the grief-stricken exhibit behaviors that may not be typical for them. While everyone's grief journey is unique, there are some common issues that people face when coping with the loss of someone close to them.

There are several studies on the stages of grief. The five original stages—see Elisabeth Kübler-Ross's book *On Death and Dying*—have been expanded to seven, twelve, or more by other academics. These are paraphrased here:

Intense Grief: Grief is a natural response to loss, and it can manifest in various ways, including sadness, anger, guilt, and confusion. The intensity and duration of grief can vary from person to person, but it's important to allow yourself to experience and process these emotions at your own pace.

Denial and Disbelief: Initially, it can be difficult to accept the reality of the loss. Denial and disbelief are common defense mechanisms that help individuals gradually come to terms with the death of a loved one. It's important to give yourself time to process the reality of the situation.

Physical and Emotional Symptoms: Grief can also manifest in physical symptoms such as fatigue, changes in appetite, sleep disturbances, and difficulty concentrating. Emotionally, you may experience mood swings, anxiety, and a sense of emptiness or numbness. Taking care of your physical and mental well-being through self-care activities and seeking support can be beneficial.

Social Withdrawal: It's not uncommon to withdraw from social activities and isolate oneself while grieving. However, isolation can hinder the healing process. It can be helpful to maintain connections with supportive friends and family members who can provide comfort and understanding.

Guilt and Regret: Many people experience guilt and regret after the death of a loved one. They may feel guilty about things they said or did not say, or have regrets about missed opportunities. It's important to remember that these feelings are a normal part of grief, and seeking support from a therapist or counselor can help you navigate them.

Financial and Practical Concerns: Dealing with the practical aspects of a loved one's death, such as funeral arrangements, legal matters, and financial issues, can add additional stress during an already difficult time. It can be helpful to seek assistance from trusted friends, family members, or professionals to help you navigate these practical matters.

Anniversary Reactions: Anniversaries, birthdays, and holidays can trigger a renewed wave of grief, as these occasions often serve as reminders of the loved one who has passed away. It's important to acknowledge and honor these emotions, and to find ways to remember and celebrate the life of your loved one.

Remember that grief is a highly individual process, and there is no "right" way to grieve. It's important to be patient and compassionate with yourself as you navigate through these common issues. If you find that your grief is becoming overwhelming or significantly interfering with your ability to function, it may be helpful to seek professional support from a therapist or grief counselor.

There are strategies and plans that can be acted on prior to a person's death that protect intended beneficiaries and make the settlement of an estate easier and less stressful, and can help promote peace and maintain healthy relationships during the inheritance process. Here are some suggestions:

Open and Transparent Communication: Encourage open and honest communication among family members about inheritance matters. This can help reduce some misunderstandings, clarify expectations, and address any concerns or conflicts early on.

Plan Ahead: The best way to minimize potential conflicts is to establish a clear and comprehensive estate plan while the individual is still alive. This includes creating a will or trust and clearly defining the distribution of assets. Seeking professional guidance from an estate planning attorney can ensure that the process is fair and legally sound. Share that information with all potential heirs.

Fairness and Equality: Strive for fairness and equality when dividing assets among beneficiaries. Consider the individual needs and circumstances of each family member and aim for an equitable distribution that takes into account their contributions and relationships.

Individual Wishes: Respect the wishes of the deceased as outlined in their estate plan. It is essential to honor their intentions and decisions, even if they may be different from what some family members expected or desired.

Focus on Relationships: Remember that preserving family relationships and maintaining peace should be the ultimate goal. Prioritize open and loving communication, empathy, and understanding. Consider the long-term impact of conflicts and work towards resolution for the sake of family unity.

Timely Distribution: Make efforts to distribute the assets in a timely manner, following the legal requirements and guidelines. Protracted delays in settling the estate can increase tensions and give rise to further conflicts. In many cases, partial distributions of estate assets, retaining enough to cover expected costs and taxes, can satisfy all the heirs—at least for a time.

Remember that every family is unique, and there may be specific dynamics or complexities that require tailored approaches. It's advisable to consult with legal and financial professionals who can provide personalized advice based on your family's circumstances.

What is the purpose of estate planning? It is certainly more than transferring a person's assets at death to the heirs or beneficiaries. But it is rare that clients address issues that potentially could complicate the legal process, impact extended family relationships, as well as cause temporary or even permanent family rifts and estrangements. Emotions can run high after the death of a loved one as described in the stages of grief discussed in the introduction.

The passing of a loved one is an emotionally challenging time for any family. Amidst the grief and sorrow, the process of distributing assets can often lead to conflicts and strained relationships among heirs. However, it is possible to navigate this delicate situation peacefully and fairly by following some essential guidelines. Explore strategies to avoid conflict among family members and ensure a smooth and equitable distribution of assets.

Clear and honest communication is the foundation of preventing conflicts among family members. To establish trust and transparency, hold a family meeting where you discuss the deceased's wishes, the assets in question, and the overall distribution plan. Encourage an open dialogue where each family member can voice their concerns and expectations. This will help everyone gain a better understanding of the situation and minimize misunderstandings.

Finally, it is crucial to have a good grasp of the legal aspects surrounding estate distribution. Depending on your jurisdiction, there may be specific laws governing inheritance and estate planning. Consulting with an attorney who specializes in estate law can provide valuable insights and ensure that the distribution process is legally sound. Having a legal framework in place can also serve as a reference point to prevent disputes.

CHAPTER 20

Equal Division May Not Be Fair

While equal distribution of assets among heirs is often the default choice, it may not always be the fairest option. Consider the unique needs and circumstances of each family member. Some may have financial stability, while others may need more assistance. To avoid conflicts, consider an equitable distribution that takes individual needs into account rather than simply dividing assets equally. Sometimes, regardless of what they say, it all comes down to money.

LEGITIMATE WANTS OR NEEDS
OF POTENTIAL HEIRS

Selecting an unbiased and neutral executor can help maintain peace within the family. An executor's role is to ensure that the deceased's wishes are carried out as per the will or the legal requirements. When a family member is chosen as the executor, it may raise suspicions of bias. Opting for a neutral third party, such as a financial adviser or a lawyer, can minimize conflicts and ensure an impartial distribution process.

Dealing with the loss of a loved one is an emotionally charged experience, and emotions can run high during asset distribution discussions. It's crucial for all family members to recognize the emotional aspect of the situation and make an effort to keep emotions in check. Encourage empathy and understanding among heirs, and remind them that the goal is to honor the deceased's wishes and maintain family unity.

Determining what is fair in terms of bequests in a will and trust is subjective and dependent on various factors. There is no true fairness since no two situations in family relationships and asset owners are alike. Here are some considerations that can help guide you in deciding what may be considered fair:

Individual Circumstances: Take into account the personal circumstances of each beneficiary, including their financial needs, existing assets, and their relationship with the testator (the person creating the will or trust). For example, if one beneficiary is financially stable while another is in significant need, you may consider adjusting the bequests accordingly.

Testator's Intent: Consider the wishes and intentions of the testator as expressed in the will or trust. The testator's desires should be given considerable weight when determining what is fair, as long as they are legally valid and not influenced by undue pressure or duress.

Equal Treatment: Fairness often involves treating beneficiaries equally, especially in the absence of specific reasons for unequal distribution. Many people choose to divide their estate equally among their beneficiaries to avoid potential conflicts or perceived favoritism.

Special Circumstances: Some beneficiaries may have special needs, disabilities, or require ongoing financial support. In such cases, it may be fair to allocate a larger portion of the estate to meet their specific requirements.

Contributions and Sacrifices: Consider any contributions or sacrifices made by specific beneficiaries during the testator's lifetime. This could include emotional support, caregiving, financial assistance, or other significant efforts that may warrant a larger bequest.

Legal Obligations: Be aware of any legal obligations or requirements imposed by local laws. Some jurisdictions have laws that protect certain family members from being completely disinherited, and failing to comply with these laws may lead to legal challenges.

Involving a financial adviser or an estate planning attorney can provide objective guidance and expertise. These professionals can offer advice on tax implications, asset management, and strategies for minimizing conflicts.

If conflicts arise that cannot be resolved through open communication, consider seeking professional mediation. A trained mediator can facilitate discussions and help family members find common ground. Mediation can be a cost-effective and efficient way to resolve disputes and maintain family harmony.

DOCUMENT EVERYTHING

To prevent future disputes and ensure transparency, keep meticulous records of all asset distribution decisions and transactions. This includes documenting the deceased's will, any changes or amendments, and records of asset transfers. Clear documentation can serve as evidence of the fairness and legality of the distribution process.

Preventing conflicts in the future begins with proactive estate planning. Encourage your loved ones to regularly review and update their estate plans to reflect changes in their assets, family dynamics, and wishes. This proactive approach can help avoid surprises and conflicts down the road.

Distributing assets among family members after the loss of a loved one can be a challenging and emotional process. However, by fostering open communication, understanding the legal framework, and prioritizing fairness and transparency, you can significantly reduce the likelihood of conflicts. Remember that maintaining family harmony is a valuable legacy that your loved one would have wanted to leave behind.

MINOR CHILDREN AS BENEFICIARIES.

When a child is an heir, what happens with their money? Children who have not reached the age of majority have limited rights in the control of their assets, even without a trust. They are in fact legally incapable of signing contracts and cannot vote. They also cannot own real estate or use the courts to sue or be sued. They do have legal rights and they can have their rights protected through the use of a legally appointed guardian and conservator under the supervision of the probate court. Their inheritance left to them in a will or trust can be held for them according to the provisions of the trust or under court supervision under the control of the court appointed conservator. Typical conditions that are attached to a child's trust include allowing the funds to be used for living expenses, education, medical care, and medical insurance, but could allow the child's trustee the discretion to distribute any funds that the trustee deems necessary or appropriate.

TRUSTEES FOR CHILDREN OR SPENDTHRIFTS

Choosing the trustee is important since that person is in a sense stepping into the role of a parent insofar as decision-making is concerned. Professional trustees, such as a bank, may refuse a request for what the child deems necessary, but which is not in fact necessary according to the professional trustee.

A case in point was one where the child's parents had passed away leaving a trust fund amounting to over four million dollars that could be distributed only for educational, medical, or living expenses at the discretion of the trustee, which was a bank trust company. The beneficiary was a college student who wanted to live off-campus in an apartment shared with three other students. She asked for enough money to buy a used car for transportation to and from college since they would be living ten miles from the university and had a schedule that varied in time and location from day to day. Despite the small cost of the car relative to the inheritance that was soon to come, the trustee refused the request, saying a car was not strictly a necessary expense since bus transportation was available. The lesson here is to choose your trustee carefully and use language that would guide a trustee on what is or is not appropriate.

Equal Division May Not Be Fair   109

Consider whether equal distribution of assets among your heirs is the best approach, or if certain beneficiaries may require more or less assistance based on their needs and circumstances. But again, what is fair is up to you. Beneficiaries do not have veto power over your decisions and are not entitled to see any of your private documents.

Question: I can't decide what to do about leaving money to my children. They are both adults and are—at the moment—self-supporting, but I worry about the future. My son has a history of bad financial management. Ten years ago, he filed bankruptcy to get rid of over $50,000 in credit card debt. He seems to have learned his lesson but now has an expensive new car, which, according to the internet, costs more than he makes in a year. I suspect he is making huge car payments. That would not be so bad but he seems to be still living way above his means. I worry that he will quickly spend any inheritance I leave him.

My daughter is a professional and is married with no children. Her husband works as a salesman and seems to make good money but changes jobs frequently. The problem is that I don't like him, and I don't want to leave her a big inheritance and then have her leave it all to him if she dies first.

Maybe I am trying to control them even after my death, but I seriously am thinking of leaving everything to charity.

Answer: Being in charge of your money from the grave is not at all unusual. Your assets are your own and you can do what you like with them. Your written will and trust are private until you die and not even your children will find out what you have done until after your death. So, you needn't worry or feel guilty about what you want to do. As time goes on circumstances might change and you can make new decisions. It is certainly possible to leave everything in trust with restrictions on when and how

(Continued . . .)

> your children can access their share. You could require payments of their share in monthly installments spread over years or held until they reach retirement age. The beauty of a trust is that you can set up any plan you want that will satisfy the issues and worries that you face. And you can make changes as you like. If the children do not approve of what you have done, they can always decline their inheritance.

The death of a loved one is made more traumatic if you leave everything regarding your estate unsettled. Dealing with all the issues that must be addressed is stressful enough without having to hire a lawyer and satisfy the family and potential heirs that you are acting properly to protect their interests as well as carrying out the intentions of the deceased.

The goal of estate planning should be more than just transferring assets from a person who has died to the heirs who should receive them. The process should also be to make the process quick, at a reasonable cost, and acceptable to the heirs. But in fact, most planning involves no planning at all. The majority of people die without a will or a trust or any other form of preparing the estate for the post-death procedures that must be followed to close out the estate.

Estate planning means creating a plan to make the disposition of assets to beneficiaries quick and seamless. It could be compared to creating a streaming television film with several episodes. There should be beginning, middle, and end, one episode leading to the next until the story is told. Our estate plan, however, should not be filled with drama and unexpected surprises. There is actually a script which, if written properly, will carry the storyline with no unexpected or surprise ending.

The first few episodes should involve identifying the specific goals of the estate plan. In most cases the goals are easily identified.

ESTATE PLANNING GOALS

- To set up a plan that involves using the estate assets to provide a lifetime income for one or more heirs.
- To ensure that all estate assets are identified, liquidated, and ultimately distributed in proper shares to the named heirs of the decedent.
- To anticipate possible contingencies that could alter the plan that was created and set up alternate plans in that case. For example, what if a named heir predeceases the will or trust maker? Or suppose there are later born or out-of-wedlock children who should be considered?
- To set up the least time-consuming and least expensive process to settle the estate of the grantor.
- To eliminate or lessen the potential hurt feelings or disagreements among the named heirs or those who are left out.
- To devise a plan of distribution for items likely wanted by more than one heir, such as heirlooms, one-of-a-kind items, and the other "stuff" that remains.

Careful planning requires that you identify all the "what ifs" and provide answers for those questions. That doesn't mean that the plan has to be exhaustively detailed. Less is more. But there should be no unanswered questions, such as "Who gets Mom's wedding ring?"

CHAPTER 21

Beneficiary Designations
for Trusts and Wills

It is not unusual for children of elderly parents to try to influence the planning decisions of their parents. In deciding how assets at death are to be distributed there are a number of commonly used formulas.

A typical beneficiary instruction is to leave everything to all the listed heirs to be divided equally among them. But most often the heirs have different needs and different sized estates of their own. Some folks try to divide the estate including tangible and intangible assets in percentages based on the perceived needs of the individual children. Others might leave out a child as an heir since they had already made substantial un-repaid loans to that child.

One area of contention is determining whether money given to a child was in fact a loan and not a gift. The character of the transfer can be clarified in the language of the trust. Sometimes there is a written loan agreement that makes it clear that the transaction was not a gift. Otherwise, we must look for evidence of the character of the money transfer. What did the deceased say to family members about the transaction? Should the loan be considered an advancement of that person's share of the total estate, or was it intended as a gift? Without evidence one way or another, a judge might have to ultimately decide.

When children try to influence the decision making insofar as how assets are to be divided, it creates a lot of stress on the parents as well as the siblings. No one wants a family rift or hurt feelings. It is important to remember that the assets do not belong to the children and that none of them have a right to inherit. As the person making the distribution decisions, you have no obligation to discuss or negotiate what you want to do. My best advice is to listen to their concerns and then say something like, "Thank you so much for your input, and I will certainly take all that into consideration when I make my decision."

You then do not have to tell them anything. Your will or trust speaks for itself, and you have no obligation to justify your decisions or share them with anyone except your attorney.

There is nothing wrong with naming your spouse as first beneficiary and then listing your children as alternates if your spouse predeceases you. But beneficiary designations can also be used to complement your estate planning or even act as a will or trust substitute.

Creating specific beneficiary conditions involves designing terms and stipulations that guide how and when beneficiaries receive benefits. These conditions can add flexibility, encourage specific behaviors, or address unique needs. Here are some inventive ideas for beneficiary conditions:

Age-Based Conditions. The most common conditional beneficiary designation is one based upon the child beneficiary attaining a certain age.

This type of beneficiary designation gives the beneficiary an option upon reaching the age of majority. She can go on to college or technical school and have it paid for by the trust, or find a job to support herself until she reaches age twenty-five. The choice would be clear for most beneficiaries and would be a way to encourage her to get an education or develop a skill.

Here are a few common examples of naming beneficiaries in a trust or will and conditions that may be satisfied by the beneficiary before they receive their full inheritance:

An unrestricted share of the estate with no conditions. This is the most common. The document may read something like

Beneficiary Designations for Trusts and Wills 115

this: "The Trustee shall apply and distribute the net income and principal of each of the shares of the resulting Trust Estate to the following Beneficiaries in the indicated fractional shares: one-half to Thomas Jones and one-half to Natisha Jones."

But what if Thomas dies before you, leaving children of his own—your grandchildren. Does Thomas's share go to Natisha, or does it go to the grandchildren? If it all goes to Natisha, we say that that share lapses. But if it goes to the grandchildren, we call it per stirpes with right of representation.

If minor children are beneficiaries, then we typically restrict their inheritance in one or more ways. A requirement that a beneficiary must attain a certain age before getting their inheritance is often done. The language regarding the distribution could be as follows:

> If any Beneficiary (including but not limited to a grandchild if any), is under the age of 25 years when the distribution is to be made, the Trustee shall retain any such property and administer and distribute the same for the benefit of the beneficiary, paying to or for the benefit of such person so much of the income and principal of the retained property from time to time, as the Trustee in his or her sole discretion deems advisable for his or her health, education, support, and maintenance.
>
> When the person for whom the property is held attains the age of 25 years, the property shall thereupon be distributed to him or her free of trust. If the person should die before attaining the age of 25, the property shall then be paid and distributed to the estate of the person and that person shall have a power of appointment to direct where that share shall go.

This provision is intended to protect a young heir's estate from their own potential mismanagement. The age can vary, and in some cases, it is paid out in installments rather than a lump sum. The practical idea is that the minor heir would have to decide to get a job or get an education. We hope that by age twenty-five they should have finished their education. Of course, these requirements and stipulations are changeable, but the changes can only be made by you. We never know what a minor heir will be like as they get older, so the document is flexible, allowing you to loosen or tighten the restrictions.

Conditions can be more than just requiring the attaining of a certain age. It could be that a potential heir has issues that could disqualify them from inheriting in your mind. Drug addiction, poor money management, estrangement from family, a genuine dislike of a person's lifestyle (or his or her spouse), or even imprisonment could justify any conditions you make. There might be requirements that an heir continue with a family business, or volunteer for a religious mission. Basically, you can attach any conditions you want since it is your money, and the heir is not required to accept it. Although I have seen very few heirs disclaim an inheritance.

Education Conditions. Benefits are distributed upon the completion of specific educational goals, such as obtaining a degree or trade or completing a certain certification such as a medical degree or a degree in economics. It's flexible and up to the grantor of the trust or owner of the asset subject to a pay-on-death provision of the asset.

The beneficiary form provided by the asset administrator may not have room to fill in all of your conditions, but you can attach them to the form as an addendum. Just be sure that the addendum is notarized.

Your beneficiary does not have to agree with the conditions you set out, and it is a good idea to have what we call an alternate beneficiary in case the original designation fails to meet the conditions. The alternate could be the trust with the asset being distributed with the residue of the trust funds.

Career Conditions. Disbursements occur when beneficiaries achieve certain career milestones, such as securing a job in their field of study or reaching a promotion level. This can be a difficult condition to fulfill and requires careful thought.

Perhaps becoming an MD or passing the state bar examination to become an attorney. This is a way to push the beneficiary into a career path that she may not like, but she can refuse. I am familiar with local families whose parents, children, and grandchildren all became attorneys; some became judges, and many joined the family law firm. They didn't have to go into law, but the opportunity was right there and seemed the obvious choice.

Community Service. Benefits are provided in exchange for completing a certain number of hours of community service or volunteer work. Again, define what organizations would be acceptable. I have seen a requirement that a beneficiary complete a religious "mission" for their church for a designated length of time prior to getting the inheritance.

Skill Acquisition. Beneficiaries must learn new skills or hobbies, such as taking art classes or learning a new language, to receive their benefits.

Performance-Based Disbursements. This one is a catch-all but could require the beneficiary to achieve personal goals; I had a client who conditioned his son's inheritance upon the son's qualifying for parole from the state prison. Other requirements might be eschewing drugs or requiring rehab.

These conditions not only create a framework for distributing benefits but also encourage beneficiaries to engage in meaningful activities, develop new skills, and contribute positively to their communities.

Beneficiary designations are a way to specify who will receive assets from certain types of accounts or policies after your death. Here are some common types:

Primary Beneficiary: The person or entity you name to receive the asset first. If you have multiple primary beneficiaries, the asset is typically divided among them according to your instructions. If a primary beneficiary dies before the grantor, that person's share could either lapse and be divided among the other primary beneficiaries or it may go to the children of the deceased primary beneficiary or to the alternate beneficiary.

Alternate Beneficiary: The person or entity who receives the asset if the primary beneficiary is unable or unwilling to accept it or who has died. They are the alternate. There might also be a tertiary beneficiary who would inherit if the primary and secondary beneficiary cannot inherit.

Revocable Beneficiary: The grantor of the trust can change this designation at any time while she is alive. This is common in wills, trusts, and many retirement accounts.

Per Stirpes Beneficiary: If a primary beneficiary predeceases you, their share is distributed to their descendants. This term means "by the branch" in Latin and ensures that the deceased beneficiary's heirs receive the benefit.

Per Capita Beneficiary: If a primary beneficiary predeceases you, their share is divided equally among the remaining primary beneficiaries. This means it doesn't go to the descendants of the deceased beneficiary but rather is redistributed among the surviving primary beneficiaries.

Specific Beneficiary: A designation where you name a specific person or entity to receive a specific asset or portion of the asset.

Class Beneficiary: A general designation where you name a class of people (e.g., "my children") rather than specific individuals. The assets are divided among members of the class. There is no requirement that the children are named since they are an ascertainable class.

Charitable Beneficiary: If you want to leave assets to a charity, you would name the charity as the beneficiary. This is often done with life insurance policies, retirement accounts, or in a will or trust. You can specify what is to be done with the charitable contribution. For example, a new roof on the church or an endowed chair at the local university.

Trust Beneficiary: You might name a trust as a beneficiary, which then directs the assets according to the terms set out in the trust document. The trust could be the alternate beneficiary in the event there are no other named beneficiaries who survive.

Understanding and selecting the right type of beneficiary designation can help ensure that your assets are distributed according to your wishes and can also have implications for estate planning considerations.

Beneficiary designations do not have to be to an individual person. You might say, for instance, that the asset to be inherited, be it life insurance, bank or brokerage accounts, or retirement funds, be distributed in unequal percentages. Perhaps ten percent each to five children and fifty percent to the Salvation Army. Some people will list dozens of percentage beneficiaries. In a case like that, an alternate or secondary beneficiary should be named in the event of the death of a primary beneficiary.

Before you just start off naming beneficiaries for all your assets that allow it, here are some basics that will educate you on necessary steps. There are multiple reasons why we would want to use a will or a trust instead of beneficiary designations. For example, those heirs who are minors, or disabled, or who rely on need-based governmental programs such as Medicaid or Supplemental Security Income should use an asset management-type will and trust so that the heir's benefit programs are not compromised. Special categories like those require more complex types of plans so that the beneficiary does not have the legal ability to manage or tap into their inheritance except as allowed by state law and within the exempt property guidelines. Their inheritance should be left in trust for them but not in such amounts as they would be disqualified from the benefit programs.

Here are the steps you can take to create a solid estate plan using one or more of the available plans. These can be used to fulfill your goals and transfer assets with the least costs and trouble available.

CREATE A PLAN USING BENEFICIARY DESIGNATIONS, A WILL, OR A TRUST (OR A COMBINATION OF THE THREE)

Consult with an attorney to draft a will and establish trusts if necessary. Wills outline how your assets should be distributed after your passing, while trusts can provide more control and flexibility in managing your assets and avoid probate as well.

A trust can be the beneficiary of your will so that if probate is necessary, the probated assets are controlled by the terms of the trust. We call that type of will a pour-over will, since the assets figuratively pour from the will to the trust. If you are married, you need to choose between individual trusts or wills or a joint trust or will. The desirability of probate avoidance using a trust will typically outweigh the benefits of a will alone.

Understand the Documents: Educate yourself on the basics of wills and trusts. Familiarize yourself with legal terms and the implications of different types of trusts, such as revocable and irrevocable trusts. If you have read this far you should have a pretty good understanding of the various documents.

Choose the Right Executor or Trustee: Select a trustworthy and responsible person to execute your will or manage your trust. This person should be willing and able to carry out your wishes efficiently. It is a very good idea to have an alternate trustee in the event your first choice is unable or unwilling to act as trustee. I recommend joint co-trustees—two or more persons, usually heirs, who act together to manage the trust assets and settle the trust. This lessens the likelihood that a non-trustee heir will cause problems and blame the trustees if there is some issue in managing assets or distributing trust funds without any oversight.

Professional trustees or trust companies are an option if you have no friends or family able to act as trustee. However, most trust companies will not accept the role unless the managed assets exceed the minimum amount they require. The compensation of the professional trustee is typically a set percentage of the total amount of dollars being managed, so they want it to make their time worthwhile based on the amount they receive. Your attorney can be the trustee, though most attorneys would decline the position.

Communicate Your Intentions: If you are comfortable doing so, discuss your estate planning decisions with your loved ones. Open and honest communication can prevent misunderstandings and potential conflicts. Keep in mind, though, that you do not need and are not required to get the permission from your heirs as to who gets what and when. Your estate is yours and not theirs. It's your money.

Consider Family Dynamics: Understand your family's dynamics, strengths, and weaknesses. This knowledge can help you plan for potential conflicts and ensure fair treatment of all beneficiaries.

Who are your beneficiaries? Look at your own situation. As touched on earlier, you might be surprised to discover that most of your intangible assets can have designated beneficiaries. Your checking account for example. Over the years I have opened dozens of checking accounts because I wanted a local bank preferably with drive-through service. To set up the accounts I met with the local branch manager, filled out some forms, chose my check style, and made my initial deposit. Later on, I designated the account to be the recipient of direct deposits and set up auto pay for recurring billings, like utilities and internet access. So, I used the accounts frequently.

I was never asked whether I wanted to name a beneficiary for my checking account. When I finally asked whether I could name a beneficiary they always said yes, then whipped out another form for me to fill out with the beneficiary's name and address. Clearly, they could do it with no trouble, but I wondered if everyone knew that a checking account could have a beneficiary. And why didn't the bank clerk suggest it to me earlier?

I learned that all sorts of deposit accounts could have beneficiaries. Things like certificates of deposit, money market accounts, brokerage accounts, and even online banking and trading accounts. Of course, nearly everyone knows that life insurance should always have a named beneficiary or several beneficiaries.

Terminology matters. The term Pay on Death (POD) refers to deposit accounts such as savings and checking accounts and certificates of deposit (CDs). Transfer on Death (TOD) is used for investment and brokerage accounts.

The people in charge of my tax-deferred accounts, like 401(k), IRAs, and other retirement accounts, did however make a point of getting my beneficiaries named, due to the availability in some cases of being able to select rollover elections and avoid penalties for mandatory minimum withdrawals. So, just ask and they will help you.

But whom should you name and under what conditions? One thing that can be done is naming multiple people or unequal shares. You could say the account would be given first to your spouse but if he/she died before you, then you could stipulate that the account be divided equally among your children. You can also include stepchildren if you like. Or leave them out if you so choose. It's your money and you can do whatever you want. You could leave the insurance or other assets to institutions, nonprofits, charities, or your next-door neighbor—literally to any one you choose; and in any amount or shares. For example, ten percent could go to the united fund and the balance to your children or stepchildren in equal or unequal shares.

It is not a good idea to just name a beneficiary and stop there.

What if your chosen beneficiary dies before you? You should have a back-up beneficiary to step in if your first choice is deceased. The contingent beneficiary could be a person, an institution, or a class of people such as "all my grandchildren" or "my surviving siblings." The idea is to not leave the replacement beneficiary role vacant, or your family will be faced with a probate court making that designation for them, and they should plan on spending a lot of face time with a lawyer.

One thing you should not do is designate your estate as beneficiary since that automatically means you are going to go through probate. In most cases that is not going to work out well for you.

If you have created a revocable living trust, the trust could be named as the beneficiary and then the trust directives as to

Beneficiary Designations for Trusts and Wills

distribution of your assets determines who gets what and when they get it and who is in charge of seeing that happens.

What if a beneficiary of a trust or probate share wants to sell their expected inheritance? Sometimes heirs do not want to wait for the estate to be distributed. They want their share now, not when probate is completed or when trust assets can be sold and distributed. There are companies which will pay a lump sum immediately for an heir's share—albeit at a sizable discount. This is not a good option in most cases since the heir would have to accept a fire sale offer to get their share in cash now.

This can be prevented in a trust-based estate settlement since a well-written trust will have language that precludes assigning, selling, or otherwise anticipating the inheritance. The heirs would also not be able to use the expectancy as collateral for a loan. This is especially important when a trust has been set up for an heir with the specific intent to manage the trust assets for his or her lifetime to be used for such purposes as providing for a lifetime income as in the case of heirs who are spendthrifts. Unfortunately, in a probate settlement there often is not a prohibition on assigning or selling your expected inheritance. Even wills rarely address that issue. This is another reason to use a trust rather than a probatable will to settle the estate. Here is the language I use in the trust or will to prevent the sale or assignment of their inheritance.

Neither the principal nor the income of the Trust shall be liable for the debts of a Beneficiary. Except as otherwise expressly provided in this Agreement, no beneficiary of any trust shall have any right, power, or authority to alienate, sell, borrow against, collateralize, encumber, or hypothecate his or her interest in the principal or income of this Trust in any manner, nor shall the interests of any Beneficiary be subject to the claims of his or her creditors or liable to attachment, execution or other process of law.

Real estate can be left to your chosen heirs with a properly drawn deed that deeds the property to them but allows you to retain the right to sell, lease, mortgage, or gift the property to whomever you choose without the permission of the ultimate grantees of the deed. The transfer of the property then would only go to them if you still owned the property at your death. This type of deed is commonly called a "ladybird deed" and has gained a lot of proponents for modest estates as a simple pro-bate avoiding transfer of the property. And in a few states the deed must be filed before your death or it is considered void. So, my recommendation is to always file the deed.

One advantage to naming your trust as beneficiary is that all assets would be put into the trust account with no probate court involvement. The trust would act as a common pot from which all expenses of administration would be paid and would have maximum ability to list any plan of distribution of estate assets that you chose. It also is easier to manage than trying to determine who would get which individual assets and their values to keep inheritances balanced among the heirs.

Spendthrift Provision

> Neither the principal for the income of the Trust shall be liable for the debts of a Beneficiary. Except as otherwise expressly provided in this Agreement, no beneficiary of any trust shall have any right, power, or authority to alienate, encumber or hypothecate his or her interest in the principal or income of this Trust in any manner, nor shall the interests of any Beneficiary be subject to the claims of his or her creditors or liable to attachment, execution, or other process of law. The limitations herein shall not restrict the exercise of any power of appointment or the right to disclaim.

It is very important that you name a beneficiary. I have had many clients take the position that they do not need to name

Beneficiary Designations for Trusts and Wills 125

one since everything was already in joint names and when their father, mother, grandmother died there was no issue with who was in charge and who got what. The lawyer took care of everything for them.

In other cases, it may be that the parents are attempting to reduce their estate and inheritance tax obligation by reducing the size of their estate with non-taxable gifts. While there is a generous exemption amount for federal estate tax, those whose estate exceeds the exemption amount would benefit greatly by gifting, However, it is not just federal estate tax that we need to plan around. Several states have their own inheritance taxes with far lower exemptions, and these may be tempered by gifting tangible or intangible assets to their heirs.

Question: My parents owned a condo in Florida and another in Arizona, but they died in Michigan, where they were legal residents and still owned the family home. Unfortunately, they did not have a trust or a will so we had to get a lawyer and go through probate, which is still not completed. I live in Michigan and my only sibling lives in Seattle. Now the lawyer says we must pay two more attorneys to do probate for the out-of-state condos. My sister is upset and thinks I made a mistake hiring the Michigan attorney and now have to do it two more times. What can I do?

Answer: "Unfortunately" is the correct word here. A court in one state does not have the authority to make decisions regarding ownership of real estate in another state. The Michigan court does have the jurisdiction to probate the Michigan real estate and transfer title, after the probate process is completed, to you and your sister. But the courts in Arizona and Florida would have to be utilized to transfer title to the properties in their states. We call the probate in the other states "ancillary probate." The cost,

(Continued...)

procedures, and length of time for the ancillary probates would depend on each state's laws.

Having a will would not have made any appreciable difference in any of the three probates. Had your parents created a trust and funded it with the real estate, there would be no probate in any of the three states, since the trust would control all property in the trust name or payable on death to the trust. It's too late now to set up a trust or use other probate avoiding methods. I cover these in my book, *How to Avoid Probate for Everyone*. You can take a lesson from your parents' lack of estate planning and have your own estate set up in a way to avoid the probate process altogether.

CHAPTER 22

The Stuff, and How to Get Rid of It

Say you now are the beneficiary and are named in the will or trust. If you are also the executor or trustee, your job is to gather together and liquidate assets; pay all expenses, taxes, and costs relating to the administration of the estate; and distribute the assets to those who are named to receive them. You would also be responsible for investing and managing the assets of a continuing trust for those not getting a full and immediate distribution of their inheritance, such as retained monies for the benefit of a minor child. Liquidating or disposing of personal tangible assets can be the most challenging part of the trust settlement, especially if the deceased was a hoarder.

I define "stuff" as the tangible personal property a person accumulates over their lifetime. Stuff like furniture, kitchenware, small appliances, soft goods (like clothing, bedding), sports equipment, tools, garden and yard items, collectibles, books, artwork—basically any tangible thing that is not real estate or vehicles.

No one wants Grandmother's china service for twelve. Heirs typically are in the middle of acquiring and storing their own stuff, so they really don't want Mom and Dad's. On the other hand, the stuff has some value—maybe not a lot—but some, so you don't want to bring in the dumpster right away. Here are some ideas on stuff disposal.

Collections. People collect things—baseball cards, salt and pepper shakers, books, ceramic figurines, sports and celebrity memorabilia, antique fishing lures, children's dolls, Star Wars

127

items—actually hundreds of types of things are subject to and are being collected. The collections are important to the collector but not so much to the collector's heirs. Sometimes the heirs will be pleasantly surprised when they find out the monetary value of the items, but most of the time they are not worth spending a lot of time trying to sell them.

When faced with collections, it is important to identify the proper way to dispose of them. Auctioneers and resale shops might be happy to take things on consignment since they do not have to put up cash in advance of sale. But it pays to look a little deeper for collections that could have significant value.

For example, I handled an estate that contained a doll collection. Not just any dolls, but antique porcelain children's dolls dating from the early twentieth century. They were found in dozens of cardboard boxes in the attic of the house. The heads on most were separated from the bodies but all the parts were there, totaling over fifty complete dolls. There were no children as heirs and the adults just wanted the most possible cash out of them.

My go-to antique dealer did not want to deal with them but pointed me to an antique doll auction business in New England. After sending digital photos of the collection, I sent the collection to them and they auctioned them off, keeping about thirty percent of the gross sales. The check from them to the estate was in excess of twenty thousand dollars. So, it was worth the effort to find the right dealer.

A similar case involved a collector who concentrated on Murano glass paperweights. Seventy-five of them went to a Detroit art auction house, which put them in their catalog, but they didn't sell. Then I discovered a company in Chicago that specialized in that type of paperweight. They took the Detroit items plus about fifty others, and the estate got a sizeable check a couple of months later.

The lesson is to find the true value of items and get them in the right hands for sale. If there are multiple heirs and someone wants a collection as part of their share, you should get several appraisals to be sure everyone is getting their fair share.

FAMILY HEIRLOOMS, ARTWORKS, ANTIQUES, AND JEWELRY

In the ideal estate, these one-of-a-kind items would have been designated in a will or handwritten list to go to particular people. Failing that, decide upon a way to either give the items to individual family members or sell them for their best value. One way is to have the heirs each take turns selecting an item, with a value assigned to each item. The goal is to have everything set aside that was individually selected and the rest disposed of in bulk. The total values of items chosen by the heirs then would be calculated and used to balance out the percentage share of total estate assets.

How do we get rid of the unselected items? That would depend on the nature of the assets and their estimated total market value. Used furniture, if not antique, typically has very little actual cash value. Some costly pieces may have little value even if in good condition and fairly new. Pool tables and upright pianos come to mind. They are heavy, difficult to move, and not in demand.

Tag sales (a.k.a. garage sales or yard sales) can get rid of some items, especially if the prices are low. Estate sales draw a lot of interest since the perception is that bargains can be had. The problem with those types of sales is that they require someone—or several people—to manage the sale. Items must be arranged by type and priced, and then you will have to haggle with potential buyers, who nearly always offer less than what you ask. It's a lot of work. There are businesses that deal in estate sales, but you have to watch out. Some will cherry pick certain items of value and sell them cheaply to their cohorts.

An estate auction is one of my go-to methods. The auction process usually results in a close figure as to the actual value of the auctioned stuff, even after deducting the auction company's percentage fee. They will also usually arrange for a dumpster to dispose of unsold items.

Some organizations will accept your items for resale, but typically do not pay you anything for the donation. They might offer a tax-deductible receipt for a charitable contribution if you ask.

FIREARMS

Firearms are a more difficult thing to handle. State and local laws can regulate the ownership and sales of firearms. An heir who wants to keep and not sell a firearm may have to store them with the police or a licensed gun dealer until an ownership permit is issued. Handguns may be more complicated to sell or assign than long guns.

Sometimes the deceased has a Federal Firearms License (FFL) and is a licensed dealer, who has ownership of what the Bureau of Alcohol, Tobacco, Firearms, and Explosives calls Class 3 firearms (including such items as silencers and some automatic weapons). These are illegal to own if you do not have the proper permits. So, guns cannot simply be handed to heirs without first being sure all proper federal and state rules and registrations have been followed.

BOOKS

Lots of people collect books. Most often they have little individual value but instead reflect the owner's interests or favorite authors. The bookstore cost of hardcover books might range from fifteen dollars to sixty dollars or more. But the moment you step outside the bookstore you would do well to get one dollar—if you can sell them at all. If you have an estate with lots of books (I have seen estates with thousands of them), you would do well to contact two or more used and antique book sellers and see if they can give you either an estimate or an offer for the lot. Don't just sell them by the piece since a buyer may be only interested in the most valuable and leave you with the rest. Try and get a price for all of them, even the paperbacks. Used books, especially bestsellers or mass market paperbacks, have little value. There is no correlation between the age of a book and its value. In other words, just because it's old doesn't make it valuable. You can try to sell your used books online one sites such as eBay and AbeBooks, but the amount of effort to catalog, photograph, and ship them may not be worth the small amount of money you receive. Contacting several local booksellers for a batch sale is likely to get you the best price.

Keep in mind that the goal is to get rid of the books, so offering them to family members might be the first step, and donating the unwanted ones to your local library or recycling center could be the last one.

BUSINESSES AS ESTATE ASSETS

Family-owned businesses and succession planning were covered earlier in this text. There are attorneys who specialize in succession planning for family-owned businesses. They can help develop agreements that protect family members when one owner dies or wants to dispose of his or her interest in the business. If the business is going to be continued after the death of one of the owners, then a way must be found to pay the deceased's estate for the value of their share of the business. This could be life insurance, or a long- or short-term payout to the estate from those who continue the business operation. Existing business taxes and debts must be considered as well as necessary licensing. Ownership of patents and trademarks may be an issue. Some businesses are worth no more than the business assets since they depend on the labor skills and reputation of the deceased owner. A one-person business like a plumber, interior decorator, or someone else who has specialized skills may not be marketable at all, although assets such as accounts receivable might be available to the estate.

TIMESHARES

Typically, timeshares are difficult, if not impossible, to sell and so have little cash value. The deceased may have paid a lot for the timeshare itself but is highly unlikely to sell it for anywhere near the initial cost. And they require annual fees as well as maintenance costs and special assessments. If an heir wants the timeshare, they should be made aware of the ongoing costs.

That said, there are businesses that will offer to sell the time-share for you, but you may be required to pay them for that service and still not get any money out of the sale.

CHAPTER 23

Do You Really Want to Be the Trustee?

What could or should be done insofar as preparing the estate in advance to make it simpler and less expensive to administer? The main thing is to encourage and assist your parents—or whomever you might be inheriting from—to make a plan now. Doing nothing at all amounts to making a decision to kick the can down the road and require that someone else clean up the mess left behind.

IT'S A JOB AND NOT A FUN ONE

Remember that as an heir, you are the one who will be paying for probate. You are the one who has to take care of funeral arrangements, cleaning out the house and garage, meeting with attorneys and accountants, handling the concerns and worries of the other heirs, and many other duties that come with settling an estate. These are not only time-consuming but involve the expenditure of a lot of money. Encouraging and helping your parents to plan will be a direct benefit to you as well as the other heirs.

One method that sometimes works is to prepare your own trust or estate plan and then tell the folks conversationally what you did and why you did it. That can open the door to a talk about wills versus trusts and suggest that advance planning is in a way a gift to their children. Offer to pay for the fees if any for attorneys. Go with them to the lawyer's office. It might

133

well be that their situation could fit into the three-pronged plan discussed in the earlier chapter (ladybird deed, beneficiary designations, and small estate procedures), so it would likely be quick and easy for them. Doing this now would save the heirs money and time in the long run.

Who is legally the one who oversees an estate after the person dies if no one was appointed by the deceased beforehand? If there is more than one child, is the oldest entitled to be in charge of the estate? It is a common misconception that being the oldest sibling automatically gives you special privileges. This may be the case in the British monarchy, but it just isn't true in real life.

Usually, the family will agree on who should be the executor or personal representative of an estate, but if there is no agreement and if more than one person wants the job, the judge assigned to the estate can appoint one of the prospective heirs or a public administrator, if no one wants the job. And it is a job. Someone has to attend to all the requirements of the estate settlement. This includes the following and maybe much more:

- Arranging for the identification of all assets and liabilities of the deceased.
- Selecting and meeting with the lawyer throughout the settlement process.
- Meeting with an accountant for tax filing purposes.
- Arranging for the sale or distribution of all the personal property including but not limited to furniture, kitchenware, family heirlooms and memorabilia, contents of basement and garage.
- The sale of the deceased's house and other property.
- Notification to all potentially interested parties, valuation of collectibles, the list goes on and on.

You are doing no one a favor by naming them to be the personal representative of the estate. It is a job, and the trustee and personal representative should keep track of the time spent and bill the estate for that time. It is likely there will be some negative feedback from one or more of the heirs. Some states automatically allow payment to the personal representative of a percentage of the estate assets as their fee, and that can be substantial. I suggest making two of the heirs co-personal representatives. The various duties can then be split up. Otherwise, you should keep a journal of every single thing done on behalf of the estate including whom you talked to, what about, and how long the conversation went on. Travel time should also be recorded.

What else needs to be done right away when a loved one dies?

CHAPTER 24

Burials and Funerals: What Is the Process?

If there had been no preplanning for funeral and burial procedures it falls upon the family to make those decisions and arrangements. Nowadays cremation has taken over inground burial due to in part the rising costs of funerals, including casket, burial plot, and the many other add-on expenses of the traditional funeral/burial. However there a lot of alternatives in many parts of the world. It is not unusual for a person to require specific procedures in writing, even when they are a bit surprising.

Here are some samples:

- In-Ground Burial: This is the most common form of burial, where the deceased is interred in a grave in a cemetery.
- Cremation: The body is cremated, and the resulting ashes, known as cremains, may be kept by the family, scattered, or interred in a cemetery.
- Mausoleum Burial: Some people choose to be buried in above-ground structures called mausoleums, often located within cemeteries.
- Natural Burial: This is an eco-friendly option where the body is buried without embalming, in a biodegradable coffin or shroud. A bare ground burial, where the body may be placed in the ground without a casket, allows for a more natural decomposition.

138   **Beneficiary Guide for Everyone**

- Burial at Sea: Some jurisdictions allow for burials at sea, subject to specific regulations to protect the marine environment.
- Other Unusual Burial Practices:
  - Cryonics: Cryonics involves the freezing of the deceased's body or brain in the hope of future revival or restoration.
  - Promession: This is a proposed method where the body is freeze-dried, pulverized, and transformed into compost that can be used for planting a tree or other vegetation. Emphasis on "proposed."
  - Space Burial: Celestial burial or space burial involves launching a small portion of the cremated remains into space.
  - Body Donation: Donating one's body to medical science or research institutions is not necessarily considered a burial practice, but it is an alternative to traditional burial or cremation.

It is essential to research and understand the local laws and regulations in your specific area regarding burial practices. Funeral directors, local government agencies, or legal professionals can provide guidance on what is permissible and what permits or licenses may be required.

The legality of burial practices varies by country and jurisdiction. Generally, there are certain regulations and guidelines that govern burial practices to ensure public health and safety. However, what is considered "typical" or "unusual" can differ depending on cultural, religious, and personal beliefs.

Assuming no estate planning had been done by the decedent, you are now faced with choosing the best legal process with which to administer the estate as well as the practical business of dealing with funerals, burial, notification of the death, securing the estate assets, and taking care of the needs of children and pets.

Burials and Funerals: What Is the Process?

These are the practical steps that need to be taken such as notification of friends and family and funeral, burial, or cremation arrangements. These things need to be done immediately; other things can wait.

Proper preparation can make the heartache of the passing of life a bit smoother. We need to be conscious of the emotional impact death has on the survivors. It is a good idea to let those close to the deceased be made aware of plans that may have been made prior to death. Prepaid arrangements may be at odds with what some may think proper or appropriate.

Ultimately, someone has to be in charge of carrying out the deceased's final wishes, if those are known, or to reach a consensus with the surviving family as to what the funerary arrangements will be. If there is a surviving spouse, that person is typically the one who makes the call as to what procedures will be followed.

Will it be a traditional funeral with a funeral home that could include embalming, a viewing of the deceased, a motorcade to a cemetery, words spoken by friends or clergy? Or is a military funeral appropriate? Perhaps a fraternal organization would be involved, such as the VFW or the Masons. There might be religious or cultural considerations and formalities that would be in order. The deceased may have made personal arrangements including such seemingly minor things as what funeral clothing in which he or she wants to be buried. Surviving minor children may need temporary to permanent accommodation. Counseling may be desirable for close friends and family. There are a lot of considerations in putting the deceased to rest.

CHAPTER 25

Now You Are a Beneficiary

Receiving an inheritance can be life-changing, and it's important to make well-thought-out decisions. Here's a general guide on what to do.

WHAT TO DO WITH YOUR INHERITANCE

- **Pause and Assess:** Take your time before making any big decisions. Allow the initial emotions to settle. Consult with a trusted adviser if needed.
- **Understand the Inheritance:** Determine what exactly you've inherited (cash, property, investments, etc.). Understanding the nature and value of your inheritance helps in making informed decisions.
- Consult Professionals:
  - **Financial Advisor:** They can help create a plan that aligns with your long-term goals.
  - **Tax Professional:** Inheritances can come with tax obligations, depending on where you live.
  - **Estate Attorney:** If you're inheriting property or complex assets, an estate attorney can ensure everything is handled legally.
- **Pay Off High-Interest Debt:** If you have any high-interest debt (like credit cards), it's wise to pay those off first. Reducing debt can relieve financial pressure.

141

- **Build an Emergency Fund:** Set aside a portion for a three-to-six-month emergency fund if you don't already have one. This will give you financial security in case of unexpected events.
- **Invest for the Future:** Consider investing part of the inheritance to grow it for the long term. You can choose from various investment options like stocks, bonds, or real estate based on your risk tolerance and goals.
- **Real Estate:** If you've inherited property, decide if you want to keep it, sell it, or rent it out. Each option has financial and personal implications. However, to better deal with tax-related issues, such as capital gains tax, it is a very good idea to have the property appraised at the time of death of the testator to preserve proof of a stepped-up tax basis.
- **Charitable Giving:** If philanthropy is important to you, you might want to donate a portion of the inheritance to causes you care about. Keep in mind that it is perfectly appropriate to direct how the charitable gift is to be used.
- **Treat Yourself (in Moderation):** It's okay to enjoy a small portion of the inheritance for something personal, whether it's a vacation or a purchase you've wanted for a long time.
- **Reassess Your Financial Goals:** This inheritance might allow you to retire early, start a business, or pursue a passion project. Review your long-term financial goals and adjust as needed.

CHAPTER 26

The Reading of the Will Ceremony

In my other books I stated that the scene we see on film and television, where the lawyer sits behind his desk in a library-like room and reads to the gathered expectant heirs the last will and testament of the deceased, is in fact a myth. There is no law requiring this ceremony and in fact it is a procedure used by few, if any, estate lawyers. But I use it occasionally in the interests of transparency and with the hope that the prospective estranged heirs will be satisfied that nothing is being hidden from them. We seek a quick and amicable settlement of the estate with everyone knowing where they stand in regard to the potential inheritance.

If you are the successor trustee or personal representative, I suggest you ask your attorney to hold such a meeting. This is in the hope that all those present will understand the procedures and time limits. Perhaps your attorney could call it a family meeting rather than a reading of the will and invite all interested parties ("interested parties" are defined as only those who are heirs in the will or trust, or who are immediate family members) to the lawyer's conference room to have the attorney lead a presentation on what is normally expected to happen in the estate. When I hold such a meeting, I make it clear that I represent the estate, not the heirs. The deceased may not have had either a will or a trust, but the meeting can still be a valuable process to educate the audience so that they will not have unrealistic expectations as to what will be done to settle the estate.

144   Beneficiary Guide for Everyone

The process of a probate or trust settlement would be explained. This explanation will include a step-by-step explanation of court procedures for probate as well as what is involved in non-probate trust settlement. The attorney would reveal who was named as the personal representative(s) or the trustee(s) by the decedent and what their role and duties will be.

The time requirements for settlement will be estimated depending upon the type of procedure that is necessary and the nature of the estate assets. This is important because people get impatient and if they aren't informed otherwise often assume that either nothing is being done or that something nefarious is happening behind their backs. We don't want them hiring their own attorney to stir up the mud.

If there are difficult assets to be administered, such as a family-owned business or out-of-state property, those will be reviewed. Copies of all the relevant documents should be provided to everyone as is allowed by state law, even the attorney fee agreement. An agenda should be provided, and the meeting quickly wrapped up with the handing out the document copies. Make it clear who is in charge—the attorney and the trustee, no one else.

The rights of the surviving spouse and minor children as well as disabled heirs have to be considered. Some states protect the rights of family to stay in the home for an extended length of time even if someone else is supposed to inherit it. Florida and Texas are good examples.

We explain the role of continuing legal guardian of minor children and who will be in charge of the inheritance of those children until they reach the age where their assets may be turned over to them. Sometimes there are conditions attached to an inheritance, such as attaining a certain age or attaining a certain educational level. (Occasionally we run into bizarre and even impossible conditions and may have to seek the guidance of a probate judge to sort it out.) The guardian oversees raising the children while the conservator is responsible for the inherited funds. Those roles can be performed by the same person,

The Reading of the Will Ceremony   145

but sometimes the roles of guardian, trustee, and conservator are different people, and the attorney should briefly describe how those roles differ and how they were selected. The nominated persons should have been informed in advance of their appointment and in some cases, the nominated person will decline to serve and the named backup or second choice steps into their place.

As to fees, detail expected court fees, inventory fees, state inheritance tax, and federal estate taxes, if any. They must understand that each telephone call or office visit by them will be recorded and billed to the estate. It is good idea to have a stenographer present at the will reading so that the meeting appears to be the formal affair that the prospective heirs expect. No brawling allowed. Make clear what will be the expenses of administration, including court costs, taxes, executor, and attorney fees and how those expenses can be minimized.

For instance, many of the things that need to be done to administer an estate are not legal in nature, but clerical. So the attorney, if there is one, should only be performing legal services. A family member may be able to perform some of the clerical administrative things at a lesser cost that the normal attorney rate.

Meeting with accountants, appraisers, and real estate agents can often be done by family members or the appointed personal representative or trustee. Explain that attorney fees and trustee/executor fees are charged by the hour and that court hearings are expensive and time-consuming. While they are entitled to each have their own attorneys, they should expect to have to pay a sizeable retainer to hire their own lawyer and those fees are not paid from the estate in most cases.

The distribution of personal property such as furniture, household goods, family heirlooms, collectibles, tools, firearms, and sports equipment and so on will be mentioned, and if the decedent left instructions as to particular items the attorney will explain when those can be transferred and what will happen to undesignated assets.

CHAPTER 27

Unfair, Weird, Unlawful, or Impossible Will Instructions

Some people personally create their own will for various reasons. They might think they are too busy, or it could be they don't want to "waste money" on a lawyer. So, they either pull out the pen and paper to write their own or go online to create one themselves. Aside from the fact that they cannot be sure that the will is done according to legally required formats or witnessing procedures, they also do not get the guidance from a legal professional as to what they can and cannot put in a will. Or they might want to put things in a will that are a problem or even impossible for their executor to carry out. The question is what can an executor do to either ignore, modify, or carry out those instructions?

HOW TO HANDLE THEM EVEN IF YOU DON'T AGREE

In most cases the personal representative of a probated will has no authority to change the instructions in the will as to who gets what and when they get it. We call these the dispositive sections of the will. The same is true of a trust or of the dispositive rules of a probate court following state law where the deceased died intestate.

However, there are situations where changes can be made. First of all, you cannot force someone to accept an inheritance. There are many reasons why someone might not want to inherit.

147

148   Beneficiary Guide for Everyone

It might be they don't need the inheritance and other heirs do. Or it may be a decision based on a poor relationship with the deceased (maybe they hated the person and want nothing from them). Whatever the reason, we can use the right to decline to inherit in full or part as a way of modifying the distribution provisions set up in the will or trust. So, while I say that trusts and wills become irrevocable at death, there is a way to make an end run around the intentions of the deceased. Sort of a loophole, you might say.

Here is a common situation: The deceased had no living spouse and three adult children. He had always favored his two daughters but had not spoken to his son in several years because he disapproved of the son's lifestyle. He left his son ten percent and everything else was to go equally to the daughters. The children had no issues with each other, and the daughters wanted to include their brother. If none of the children had children of their own, they could each do a partial disclaimer so that the shares of all three would equalize. That is because of language normally written in wills and trusts which says in effect that if a named heir dies before the deceased, then that share is to go to that person's children if any and if there are none, to the other heirs at law of the deceased.

In this situation using a simple example, if there was a total estate to distribute of $240,000, then each daughter would get $108,000 and the son $24,000. If each daughter disclaimed $28,000, then each of the three would end up with $80,000. The reason is that the amount disclaimed by each daughter would be divided equally between the other daughter and the son. So the son gets his $24,000, plus $28,000 from each sister totaling $80,000. Each daughter gives up a net amount of $28,000 (each daughter gives up $56,000 but inherits $28,000 from each other leaving each child with $80,000).

If there is a trust that will continue for the benefit of certain heirs, who will be in charge of that trust? It may not be the same person who is in charge of the deceased's estate.

Unfair, Weird, Unlawful, or Impossible Will Instructions 149

Finally, who are the heirs according to the will, trust, or state law depending upon which documents were actually created by the deceased?

A copy of the dispositive documents would then be given to each interested party, and they will be told that copies of all court documents and correspondence will be copied to them, preferably via email. A short handout on everything you explained is also helpful so long as the attorney uses the proper disclaimers to avoid someone interpreting his statements in the meeting as specific legal advice.

Transparency is vital to a drama-free estate settlement. It is entirely understandable that when an interested party is told nothing about the state of progress of an estate and as a lot of time passes that they would think having their own attorney would be a very good idea. But unless there is actually some identifiable misfeasance or malfeasance going on, having one or more additional attorneys involved is only going to make the estate take longer, cause a lot of suspicion and distrust, and cost more money.

Question: Is there some way I can set up my will or trust so that no one can embezzle from it?

Answer: No. We cannot guarantee there would be no embezzlement, but we can do a lot of things that would make it more difficult. First, we could require probate oversight of the will or trust. This would require court approval of investments, expenses, and fees charged against the estate. We could also ask the court to require the trustee or personal representative to post a performance bond. The downside is that we normally want to avoid probate court involvement if at all possible, so that technique would result in greatly increased costs particularly for attorney and executor fees. There are other ways that work that still avoid probate.

(Continued...)

You could name a professional trustee or trust adviser to oversee the settlement of the estate, particularly if you are dealing with a trust-based estate plan. The trust adviser would have the ability to supervise a trustee or even to remove a trustee from management decisions over the trust assets.

CHAPTER 28

Pet Trusts

Contrary to what some people think, your fur baby dog or cat is not a person, and you cannot make your pet an heir since it cannot hold title to assets. It is not a person. You can, however, leave funds in trust under the management of a human or corporate trustee for the care of your pets. Pet trusts are legal arrangements designed to provide for the care and maintenance of pets in the event of the owner's death or incapacity. The legality of pet trusts can vary depending on the jurisdiction, as laws pertaining to trusts and animals can differ from one country or state to another. However, pet trusts have gained recognition and acceptance in many jurisdictions.

PETS CAN BE BENEFICIARIES TOO

Generally, pet trusts are created by including provisions in a legally valid trust document that specify how the pet should be cared for and provide funds for the pet's well-being. These conditional trusts typically designate a trustee who will be responsible for managing the trust assets and ensuring that the pet's needs are met according to the instructions set forth in the trust.

Many jurisdictions have enacted specific statutes or laws that explicitly recognize and regulate pet trusts. These laws may outline the requirements for creating a pet trust, specify the permitted duration of the trust, determine the permissible uses of trust funds, and establish mechanisms for enforcing the trust's terms.

It is important to consult the laws of your specific jurisdiction or seek legal advice to understand the exact requirements and limitations surrounding pet trusts in your area.

The pet trust can be a standalone document or can be contained within the language of your own revocable living trust. Be sure to tell the named trustee of the pet trust of their appointment as such and give them a copy of the pet trust provisions. Here are the important points you should include in forming your pet trust:

1. Identify by name and breed your covered pets. Given the life expectancy of pets, specify if this pet trust applies to all pets that you own at your death or only the ones you have specifically named in the trust.
2. Who is the caretaker responsible for taking care of the pets? Include their name and address.
3. Add a second and even a third caretaker choice with contact information.
4. Specify the amount of money that will be set aside to fund the pet trust after your death. This should include an estimate of costs for food, grooming, and medical care as well as compensation to the caretaker. A set amount should be enough that the pets can be paid out of the income earned by the trust fund with the ability to draw on the principal as well in unexpected situations.
5. Compensation of the caretaker is typically a set amount per week, month, or year with a set-aside amount equal to ten years or more to be held in the trust account.
6. The pet trust will cease at the death of all pets. Any residue of unused income and principal should then be turned over to an organization of the trust settlor's choice.
7. The disposition of deceased pets' remains should be determined, whether that be burial or cremation and if buried, the facility where the burial takes place.

8. Identify the veterinarian (name and address) customarily used to care for the health of the pets. Is the caretaker required to continue to use this veterinarian or can the caretaker choose another veterinarian?

9. If you have more than one pet at the time of your death, has the caretaker agreed to take care of all of them, and if not, who would take care of the other pets?

10. Is there an organization, such as a no-kill shelter, that you would agree to use as a caretaker of last resort if your initial choices are unable or unwilling to accept responsibility as caretaker?

11. You may want to include a letter of instruction that the pets shall live in the home of the caretaker and treated in the same manner as you have been providing them. This should include details as to your wishes, such as to being in a home where there are no other animals that could endanger the pet, or that the pet should receive regular human interaction and not be left alone for extended lengths of time.

12. The letter of instruction may contain information on eating schedules, food allergies, and regular scheduled medical care and exercise.

13. Medical care shall include dental care, medications, and emergency care due to accidents or illness.

14. The trustee shall have all the powers specified in the original trust document wherein the pet trust was created and as authorized and set forth in the laws of the state of residence of the pet caretaker.

CHAPTER 29

Preserving and Accessing Digital Assets

Estate planning for digital assets is becoming increasingly important in our digital age. Digital assets can include everything from online bank accounts to social media profiles, digital photographs, and cryptocurrency. Here's a guide to help you plan for the management and transfer of your digital assets:

Identify Your Digital Assets. Begin by making an inventory of all your digital assets. These may include:

- Financial accounts: Online banking, PayPal, Venmo, investment accounts.
- Cryptocurrency: Bitcoin, Ethereum, wallets, and exchange accounts.
- Social media: Facebook, Instagram, Twitter, LinkedIn.
- Email accounts: Gmail, Outlook, etc.
- Subscriptions: Netflix, Amazon, Spotify, etc.
- Digital media: Photos, videos, documents stored on the cloud (e.g., Google Drive, Dropbox).
- Websites and domain names: Personal blogs or e-commerce sites.
- Online stores: Accounts on eBay, Etsy, etc.

List Your Login Information. Keep a secure list of your usernames, passwords, and answers to security questions for

155

each account. Use a password manager to securely store this information, which can be shared with a trusted person.

Designate a Digital Executor. In many jurisdictions, you can appoint a digital executor, a person responsible for managing your digital assets after you pass away. This individual can:

- Access and close your accounts.
- Manage online payments, subscriptions, and cloud services.
- Ensure that sensitive data is handled according to your wishes.

Include Digital Assets in Your Estate Plan. Explicitly mention digital assets in your will or trust and provide instructions on how they should be handled.

Legal Permissions. Ensure your digital executor has the legal right to access your digital accounts by including language that complies with the Revised Uniform Fiduciary Access to Digital Assets Act (RUFADAA) in your documents.

Transfer of Ownership. For some digital assets (like cryptocurrency), make sure you have clear instructions on how to transfer ownership.

Backup Important Digital Assets. Ensure critical digital files, such as family photos or important documents, are backed up on physical drives, as some platforms may delete accounts after a certain period of inactivity.

Review Terms of Service Agreements. Different platforms have various rules about what happens to an account after the owner passes away. For example, Facebook allows you to designate a legacy contact to manage your memorialized account. Google has an Inactive Account Manager tool that can automatically share access with a trusted contact after a period of inactivity.

Plan for Cryptocurrency and NFTs. Ensure your executor has access to the private keys and instructions for transferring these assets. Write down wallet recovery phrases and store them securely, either in a safe or with a trusted individual.

Keep Your Plan Updated. As your digital presence changes, update your estate plan and password lists to reflect new accounts and subscriptions.

Provide Instructions for Handling Social Media and Personal Data. Decide whether you want your social media accounts memorialized, deleted, or managed in another way after your passing.

CHAPTER 30

Settling the Estate

The term "settling the estate" refers to the period immediately after the death of one or both spouses. Settling an estate in a living trust is generally very easy. If all of the assets are in the living trust and if the estate has been organized, settling the estate typically takes less than an hour.

UPON DEATH

1. Make important telephone calls;
2. Make funeral arrangements, including memorial or flowers and funeral notice;
3. Notify other people;
4. Check the safe-deposit box and checking accounts;
5. Make an appointment to meet with your primary adviser, financial planner, attorney, accountant, etc.; and
6. Apply for a Tax Identification Number, if necessary.

Military Papers. Copies of military discharge papers should be obtained. If an individual who served in the armed forces dies, the Veterans Administration will provide $150 toward funeral expenses, a headstone marker, and an American flag, if desired.

In the process of making funeral arrangements, you will need to take the military separation papers to the funeral home. These papers are needed to show proof that the deceased person was a veteran of military service.

160 Beneficiary Guide for Everyone

Order Death Certificates. Order at least ten death certificates. A separate death certificate will be needed for each insurance policy and each real asset (real estate, stocks, bonds, and so on) that you desire to ultimately sell or transfer. A simple copy of the death certificate is not sufficient; it must be a certified copy, obtained from the county or parish recorder's office. Unfortunately, certified copies of the death certificate are seldom available until about ten days after the death of an individual. However, you can usually obtain one or two copies of the death certificate for immediate use directly from the funeral home. With a copy of the living trust and a certified copy of the death certificate, the surviving trustee or successor trustee then has exactly the same power to manage the estate as the deceased individual had while living.

Check Safe-Deposit Box and Checking Accounts. In the early 1970s, the death of a spouse could have drastically limited the surviving spouse's ability to gain access to funds needed for daily subsistence. The primitive practice of immediately locking up the safe-deposit boxes and the checking accounts of deceased individuals no longer exists. Now, upon the death of a spouse or parent, neither the checking account nor the safe-deposit box is inaccessible.

You should look in the safe-deposit box for two reasons. First, the deceased may have left a message or a statement of posthumous desires that should be carried out by the survivors. The second, and more important, reason to look in the safe-deposit box is to inventory the contents to be sure that all of the valuable assets (such as real estate deeds and stocks and bonds) are in the name of the trust.

As a good business practice, it is worthwhile to put your safe-deposit box in the name of your living trust. With the trust document and a death certificate in hand, the bank should readily give the successor trustee access to the safe-deposit box. In your estate-planning process, do not forget to let your successor trustee know where your safe-deposit box is located, as well as the location of the key to the safe-deposit box.

Settling the Estate

Make Appointment With Your Primary Adviser. The next step is to make an appointment to meet with your primary adviser. The actual settlement process, involving the estate and financial affairs, will begin at the meeting with this person.

THE SETTLEMENT PROCESS

If you have done your estate planning properly and if you have all of your assets in the living trust, your survivors have nothing to do from a legal standpoint. They do not have to change your trust or change title to any of your assets. The one exception would be, upon the death of a single individual or the second spouse (if married), when the estate is large enough to be subject to federal or state taxation.

The surviving spouse or adult children should be able to settle the estate without difficulty, so long as it has been organized. The surviving trustee or successor trustee needs only a copy of the death certificate and a copy of the living trust to allow him or her to take whatever action is necessary on behalf of the trust.

The following steps should be followed by your primary adviser to settle an estate in a living trust:

1. Review the instructions in your living trust document;
2. Notify life insurance companies;
3. Ensure that all assets are inside the trust;
4. Review the size of the estate;
5. File an income tax return;
6. Obtain a written valuation of assets;
7. Review business agreements;
8. Review credit cards;
9. Distribute personal effects; and
10. Review allocation and distribution of assets.

Give copies of the trust and accounting of trust receipts and disbursements to all interested parties. These are the named heirs and their legal representatives.

Review the Trust Instructions. The importance of organizing your estate is especially apparent during the process of estate settlement. By organizing the estate, it prevents a guessing game upon the death of a grantor/settlor. Having an organized estate allows the survivor the privilege of settling the estate in minutes (or possibly an hour), rather than trying to piece together the assets in the estate over several months.

You and your primary adviser should specifically look at the following sections of the living trust document:

1. The actual trust, specifically the section covering the "successor trustee" for authority in administering the trust. Also, the section covering allocation and distribution to find out the desires of the deceased person.
2. The special directives section of the trust to distribute specifically named tangible assets to those who are to receive them.

If the successor trustee is the surviving spouse, the trust provides that he or she has exactly the same power to administer the trust as before the death of the spouse. Now that only one of the original trustees is still living, it is most important to be sure that the trust names competent successor trustees to assume responsibility for the trust upon the eventual death of the second spouse.

Notify Life Insurance Companies. Your adviser should check to be sure that each of the life insurance companies has been notified of the death of the insured. Each insurance company will require a certified copy of the death certificate.

Ensure Assets Are Within the Trust. Your adviser should help you ensure that all of the assets are within the trust or have the trust named as a beneficiary. If any assets are not in the trust and the value of all assets outside the trust exceeds the value established by the particular state for probate, then the assets outside the trust must go through probate. If everything is in the trust, the surviving trustee steps in immediately and, with the trust and a death certificate, has identically the same power to buy, sell, or transfer any of the assets as did the individual who placed those assets into the trust.

Review Size of Estate. The adviser should check the information to determine whether the estate is subject to federal estate taxes and state inheritance taxes. If so, the adviser should ascertain which forms need to be filed and how much tax needs to be paid.

With proper estate planning, there need not be any estate taxes to pay upon the death of the first spouse, regardless of the size of the estate. However, if estate taxes are due, a Form 706 (Federal Estate Tax Form) must be filed, and any taxes due must be paid within nine months of death. There are options available under the tax code for extending estate tax payments over a period, often years, but most estates do not qualify for the extension.

Many states are now conforming to the federal estate tax code to the extent that, if no federal estate tax is due on an estate, then no state inheritance tax is due. However, there are states which have retained the inheritance tax, so be sure to ask your adviser about that. Since each state is different, the particular state laws for inheritance taxes need to be checked at the time of death.

File Income Tax Returns. Upon the death of a spouse, the adviser should explain that the surviving spouse has a right to file a joint income tax return (Form 1040, as had been done while the spouse was alive) for the year in which his or her spouse died. The surviving spouse should keep an accurate record of the decedent's last medical and funeral expenses because the medical expenses can be deducted from the survivor's taxable income, and the funeral expenses can be deducted for estate tax purposes.

A surviving spouse acting as the surviving trustee will typically pay out all the income from the trust to himself or herself and continue to report the trust income on his or her personal Form 1040 income tax.

164   **Beneficiary Guide for Everyone**

Upon the death of both spouses or a single person, the entire living trust becomes irrevocable. Depending upon the distribution instructions, income may or may not be retained in the trust. In either case, however, the successor trustees of the trust must then file a Form 1041S income tax return. For example, if the trust were providing for minor children, possibly only a portion of the trust income would be distributed to the children. The children would be responsible for reporting the income they received from the trust on their own individual income tax returns, and the trust would be responsible for paying taxes on any income that was retained in the trust.

Any assets retained in trust must use the special IRS Trust Identification Number. The practice of using this number after the death of the grantors/settlors is logical, because the social security numbers belonging to the grantors/settlors cease upon their deaths.

If the trust has retained earned income, it may be required to pay federal income taxes. On the other hand, if all of the income is paid out from the trust, then the recipients of the income will report such income on their own Form 1040 tax returns and pay any taxes due. The trust must still file a Form 1041S Trust tax return. However, as previously mentioned, if all of the income of the trust is paid out, then the trust has no taxable income to report on Form 1041S.

It may be to your tax advantage to retain some income in the trust. Even though the 1986 tax code eliminated the income tax advantages of retaining income in the decedent's irrevocable half of the trust and having it act as a separate tax entity, Congress continues to change the tax laws. Therefore, your tax attorney or CPA should review the pros and cons of whether to use the irrevocable trust as a separate tax entity.

Obtain Written Valuation of Assets. The adviser should explain that one of the most important functions that must be completed upon the death of an individual who has a living trust is to establish written valuation of all of the assets in the trust. It is absolutely necessary to obtain written valuation of all real estate and securities in order to determine a new cost basis for these assets and to take advantage of stepped-up valuation, thus minimizing the taxable gain when the assets are eventually sold.

The adviser should describe why and how to get stepped-up valuation. It is essential to establish a written valuation of each asset upon the death of a grantors/settlors. The written valuation provides a valid and documented justification of the asset's current market value for determining stepped-up valuation.

The best method of valuing real estate and one that is not likely to be challenged by any tax authority is getting a written appraisal by a certified real estate appraiser. You will have to pay for this, but it is a worthwhile trust expense. You can use real estate broker appraisals, but these are subject to challenge.

It is most important to place these written valuations in your living trust book (or somewhere else safe and accessible), so that you may use the valuations to substantiate your new stepped-up cost basis to the Internal Revenue Service, possibly years later, when you decide to sell your real estate. You must be able to prove your cost basis in writing.

The same principle of establishing written proof of current market valuation at date of death applies to any real estate and to any survivor, whether a surviving spouse or children. Note that your children also get stepped-up valuation as their cost basis upon the death of the surviving spouse.

Establishing the current market value of stocks and bonds is very simple; just look on the internet by searching for the stock name and date of death. The stock and bond quotations on or near the date of death are sufficient.

Alternatively, most brokers will provide these figures to you in writing if you ask them to do so. In many cases, a monthly statement of account from a brokerage firm will include the value as of the date of the statement. Remember, the market value of the stocks and bonds at date of death becomes the new cost basis, which will be used to compute any taxable gain when the assets are eventually sold.

Review Business Agreements. Your adviser should review business agreements for action, dispositions, and benefits. Any businesses must be valued very carefully and wisely. You should hire at least two, possibly three, certified public accounting firms to value your business. Since most privately held businesses have a minimal cost basis, stepped-up valuation can become extremely important. However, you must establish a sound and justifiable basis to satisfy the Internal Revenue Service. There are business valuation experts who can also give a very good and logical valuation for you.

When you have an interest in a business of substantial value, you should be aware that a number of estate planning tools can be used to freeze or establish the value of the business and, if desirable, to shift the gain to your children. The various alternatives should be pursued with a knowledgeable estate planning attorney. Strategies such as family limited partnerships or gifting can dramatically reduce your estate tax for various kinds of assets.

The IRS has several methods by which to compute corporate valuation, and upon your death, the IRS will always strive to come up with the highest valuation for your business. For your valuation purposes, the IRS looks at a business the day before an individual dies, not the day after. Thus, where there is an interest in a privately held business, a proper estate plan is essential. While you are living, being the most knowledgeable about your business, you are in the best position to do something toward determining a proper valuation. Failure to do so may have a tragic result.

Review Credit Cards. The next step to take in settling an estate is to review the credit cards that were issued to the deceased individual and to determine whether they should be destroyed. Cards that should definitely be destroyed are those issued only in the name of the deceased or for business use only.

Distribute Personal Effects. At this time, it is appropriate to distribute personal effects as specified in any special directive. Any special estate distributions should also be made, if specified. Your adviser should help you begin this step by checking the section titled "Special Directives" in your revocable living trust.

Review Allocation and Distribution. If assets are to be distributed or retained in trust for the heirs, your adviser should help you determine which assets and real estate should be distributed, sold, or converted to income. Remember, though, to first determine any outstanding debts or taxes that must be paid before the estate is distributed.

The importance of the allocation and distribution aspects of settling an estate cannot be overemphasized. The "Allocation and Distribution" section of the trust should be reviewed carefully. Even if only one spouse has died, the decedent may have left specific instructions as to certain assets that are to be distributed outright upon his or her death. Since the trustee should be given the choice of distributing in cash or in kind (by the language in the trust), the trustee preferably should distribute the assets outright, rather than selling them and then distributing the cash.

If the decedent was unmarried or the surviving spouse, then the allocation and distribution of the assets in the estate must conform to the "Allocation and Distribution" section of the trust. Again, it is always preferable to distribute the assets, where appropriate, rather than simply selling the assets and then distributing cash. On the other hand, to be perfectly fair to all heirs, it is often difficult to divide assets equally, so it may be necessary to sell some assets and then distribute equal dollar amounts in cash to each heir.

Final Issues. After the survivor has met with the primary adviser, he or she still has several months within which to take care of some important issues: Making sure assets are most advantageously placed into the various trusts, reviewing the way these assets are invested, and filing Form 706 for estate taxes, if required.

Review Investments and Investment Objectives. Review the investments in the trust to see whether they meet the objectives of income, growth, and security. Determine whether some assets should be reinvested to provide adequate income as well as appropriate growth for a hedge against inflation. The assets should be reviewed at least annually by a certified financial planner.

Upon the death of an individual, it makes sense to review the types of investments in the estate to see whether they still correspond with the objectives of the survivors. This review is particularly necessary when the survivor is a spouse, a minor child, or individual of any age with a disability. Typically, upon the death of a spouse or a parent, the family income is reduced substantially. It may be far more appropriate to sell assets that were invested for growth and to replace them with income-producing assets.

On the other hand, if both parents are deceased, the beneficiaries of the trust are the children, and the children are to receive the assets with an outright distribution, then the simplest way to distribute the assets is just to change title to the assets. However, if the assets are to be retained in trust for a period of time, if may be more appropriate to leave the assets invested for growth.

As mentioned earlier, if part or all of the living trust becomes irrevocable and assets are retained in the trust, it will be necessary to annually file a Form 1041S Trust tax return for the irrevocable part of the trust.

If the death was, or could have been, the result of another person's negligence, such as medical malpractice or an auto accident, contact your attorney to see what benefits may be available for the family.

It is now required in Michigan and some other states that the trustee publish notice of the death of the grantor to potential creditors and allow them four months to present claims against the trust estate. This creates a short statute of limitations on unknown claims against the grantor so that claimants cannot come back to the trustee after the four-month period is up and expect payment. This does not apply to known creditors but is a great advantage in finalizing the trust against possible unknown claims. A notice is published one time in a newspaper of general circulation in the county where the grantor resided.

APPENDIX

Fiduciary Act: Powers of the Law to Control Wayward Trustees

ESTATES AND PROTECTED INDIVIDUALS CODE (EXCERPT)
Act 386 of 1998
700.1308 Breach of duty; remedies; order for accounting.
Sec. 1308.

1. A violation by a fiduciary of a duty the fiduciary owes to an heir, devisee, beneficiary, protected individual, or ward for whom the person is a fiduciary is a breach of duty. To remedy a breach of duty that has occurred or may occur, the court may do any of the following:
   a. Compel the fiduciary to perform the fiduciary's duties.
   b. Enjoin the fiduciary from committing a breach of duty.
   c. Compel the fiduciary to redress a breach of duty by paying money, restoring property, or other means.
   d. Order a fiduciary to account.
   e. Appoint a special fiduciary to take possession of the estate's, ward's, protected individual's, or trust property and administer the property.
   f. Suspend the fiduciary.
   g. Remove the fiduciary as provided in this act.

172   **Beneficiary Guide for Everyone**

    h.   For a fiduciary otherwise entitled to compensation, reduce or deny compensation to the fiduciary.

    i.   Subject to other provisions of this act protecting persons dealing with a fiduciary, void an act of the fiduciary, impose a lien or a constructive trust on property, or trace property wrongfully disposed of and recover the property or its proceeds.

2.   In response to an interested person's petition or on its own motion, the court may at any time order a fiduciary of an estate under its jurisdiction to file an accounting. After due hearing on the accounting, the court shall enter an order that agrees with the law and the facts of the case.

Glossary

BENEFICIARY: One for whose benefit the living trust is created and funded.

CONSERVATOR: A person who has the legal duty to care for and maintain the property/assets of an incapacitated adult or minor child.

DECEDENT: A person who has died.

ESCHEAT: The legal process in which property or assets are transferred to the state when a person has no will or heirs.

ESTATE TAXES: The taxes imposed by the federal government on the transfer of assets at death. Estate taxes are generally paid by the personal representative of the probate estate or the trustee of a living trust. This is in addition to inheritance tax imposed by some states.

EXECUTOR: The person who is appointed by the probate court to administer a probated estate. If the person is female, the term Executrix was once widely used. See personal representative below as modern usage. The title Administrator is sometimes used in an intestate estate.

FIDUCIARY: The obligation to manage assets in the same way a prudent person would manage his own assets.

GRANTOR/SETTLOR: Parties who establish a trust by transferring property to an appointed trustee to be managed and/or distributed for the benefit of another.

GUARDIAN: The person who has been appointed by a court to care for and maintain the person and/or property of a minor child or disabled adult.

HEIR: A person who inherits property (according to state law scheme of distribution).

INTESTATE: A situation where a person dies without leaving a valid will.

ISSUE: Lineal descendants of all degrees (e.g., children, grandchildren, great-grandchildren).

JOINT TENANCY: A co-ownership of property by two or more parties in which each owns an undivided interest that passes to the other co-owners on his or her death (known as the "right of survivorship").

LIFE TENANT: A trust beneficiary whose interest consists solely for the use of, and income flow from, the trust funds during his lifetime.

LIVING TRUST: A legal entity established by means of a written trust agreement during the lifetime of the creator of the trust. The terms of the trust agreement govern the operation of the trust funds.

PAY ON DEATH (POD) OR TRANSFER ON DEATH (TOD): A directive by a person to a broker or bank to pay or transfer assets to named beneficiaries at the time of the owner's death without probate.

PERSONAL REPRESENTATIVE: The person or institution who is appointed by the testator or testatrix in his or her will to take care of the funds and property after death (also referred to as the "personal representative" of the estate). The personal representative functions under the jurisdiction of the probate court.

PROBATE: The legal proceeding by which the probate court is given full jurisdiction over the assets of the decedent. Probate starts with the filing of the decedent's will with the probate court and ends after all taxes and debts of the decedent have been paid and the assets accounted for distributed in accordance with the terms of the decedent's will. Probate usually lasts for at least six months and can endure for two years or more.

QUALIFIED DOMESTIC TRUST: A trust that meets the conditions defined in Section 2056A of the Internal Revenue Code as required to qualify a trust established for the benefit

Glossary

of a surviving spouse who is not a United States citizen for the federal estate tax marital deduction.

REVOCABLE LIVING TRUST: A living trust governed by a trust agreement whose terms may be amended, modified, or otherwise revoked by the grantor during his lifetime.

TENANTS IN COMMON: Two or more people who each own an undivided interest in a titled asset.

TENANTS BY THE ENTIRETIES: A married couple who own real estate jointly with rights of survivorship. Similar to joint tenants with right of survivorship (JWROS) who are not married.

TESTATE: Dying with a valid will as opposed to INTESTATE dying with no valid will.

TESTATOR: A person who makes a will.

TRUSTEE: The person or institution who is responsible for holding, managing, and distributing money and other property contributed to the living trust for the exclusive use and benefit of the beneficiaries.

Index

A

accounting, as legal right of beneficiaries, 93

Act 386 of 1998, 171–172

Adult Protective Services, 87

age-based beneficiary conditions, 111

agents, 19, 20, 21

alternate beneficiary, 118

amendment, trust protector and, 26

anniversary reactions, loss, grief, and, 100

annuity contracts, 2

antiques, getting rid of, 129

appendix, 171–172

art works, getting rid of, 129

asset exclusion, irrevocable Medicaid trusts and, 54

asset management, 53–54, 60, 107

asset protection

    durable power of attorney and, 19–23

    irrevocable beneficiaries and, 8

    Medicaid trust and, 53, 56

assets. *See also* asset protection; digital assets

    businesses as estate, 131

    distribution of, 7–11, 107

    equal distribution of, 30–31, 105–111

    estate and, 1–5

    investment, transfer at death of, 67

    joint, 16

    from previous marriages, naming heirs and, 30

    separate, revocable trust and, 14

attorney-in fact, 19

attorneys. *See* lawyer consultation

B

bank accounts, beneficiary designation and, 67

bankruptcy, in partnership business, 49

beliefs, naming heirs and, 30–31

beneficiaries. *See also* beneficiary designations; heirs; irrevocable beneficiaries; revocable beneficiaries

    back-up or contingent, 122

    conditions, ideas for, 114–119

    debts of, 123, 124, 141

    defined, 173

    equal treatment of, 32

    inheritance and decision guidelines, 141–142

    irrevocable, 7

    kinds of, 5

    legal rights of, 93–97

    minor children as, 107–108

    naming, 121–122, 124–125

    revocable, 7

    using percentages to treat, 68

beneficiary deed, 59

beneficiary designations

    benefit of carefully prepared, 80, 99

    common types of, 117–119

    court challenges to, 81

    defined, 5

    estate planning using, 67–68

    power of attorney and, 20

    reversing, 89

    revocable, 8

    setting up irrevocable, 7

    of trusts and wills, 113–126

blended family, revocable trust and, 14

body donation, 138

books, getting rid of, 130–131

breach of duty, remedy of, 171–172

burial at sea, 138

burials and funerals

    legality of burial practices, 138

    practical steps for, 139

177

178 Beneficiary Guide for Everyone

samples and unusual practices,
137–138
traditional, religious or military, 139
businesses, as estate assets, 131
buyout, valuing, 48

C

career, as beneficiary condition, 116–117
caregiver support, Medicaid trusts
and, 56
care management, Medicaid trust
and, 54
certainty and security, irrevocable
beneficiaries and, 8
challenge, as legal right of
beneficiaries, 93–94
charitable beneficiary, 118
charitable giving, 142
checking account, settling estate and
locking up, 160
children. *See also* minor children
influencing decision making of
assets, 113–114
trustees for, 108–110
claim support, gathering evidence to,
90
class beneficiary, 118
collections, getting rid of, 127–128
communication, as strategy prior to
death, 101
community service, as beneficiary
condition, 117
compensation, of trust protector, 26
complexity, irrevocable beneficiaries
and, 9
conflict resolution, 27, 40–41, 71,
79–80
conservator, 144, 145, 173
consultation. *See* lawyer consultation
contributions and sacrifices of
beneficiaries, considering, 106
control, revocable beneficiaries and, 8
co-personal representative, 135
corporation, trust and, 15
costs, contesting a will and, 91
co-trustees, naming, 37–38, 39–40
"cottage trusts," 36
courts, Will contest and following
decision of, 92
credit card payments, heirs and, 88
creditor claims, revocable beneficiaries
and, 8

credit union accounts, beneficiary
designation and, 67
cremation, 137
customer list, valuing, 48–49
Cyronics burial, 138

D

death
distribution of assets after, 7–11
end of Social Security and, 87–88
ladybird deed and transfer on, 61
life insurance proceeds at, 1–2
ownership at time of, 1
person overseeing estate after,
134–135
power of attorney after, 20
recording ladybird deed before,
60–61
strategies prior to, 101–103
death certificates, settling estates and,
160
debt, of beneficiary, 123, 141
deceased, ignoring wishes of, 43–45
decedent, defined, 173
deed, beneficiary, 59
denial and disbelief, loss, grief, and, 100
digital assets
backup of, 156
defined, 155
designating digital executor, 156
identifying, 155
in estate plan, 156
keeping updated plan, 157
legal permissions, 156
login information, 155–156
planning for cryptocurrency and
NFTs, 156
providing instructions for social
media and personal data, 157
reviewing terms of service
agreement, 156
transferring of ownership, 156
directed trustee, 25
disability
in partnership business, 49
planning for, 1
power of attorney and, 21
disabled heirs, revocable trust and, 14
disputes
attorney assistance in mediating, 71
conflict resolution, 40–41
trust protector and resolving, 27

Index

distributions
of assets after death, 107
of assets in prior to death, 102
as legal right of beneficiaries, 93
distribution trustee, 25
divorce action, in partnership business, 49
documentation and disclosure, Medicaid trusts and, 55
documents
for ensuring transparency, 107
losing, 96–97
preparation for legal purposes, 71
understanding, 120
drafting and execution of will, contesting will and, 83
drama-free estate settlement, 149
durable power of attorney documents, 32–33

E

education, as condition for beneficiary, 116
emergency fund, building, 142
emotional impact, contesting a will and, 91–92
emotions
after death, 102
during asset distribution discussions, 105
in check, naming heirs and, 31
employees obligations, in partnership business, 49
enhanced life estate deed. *See* beneficiary deed
environmental protections, as beneficiary, 5
equal distribution of assets, 105–111
guidance on fair decisions, 105–107
equal treatment
of beneficiaries, 106
naming heirs and, 32
equal *vs.* fair, in naming heirs, 30
equitable distribution, in naming heirs, 30–31
escheat, defined, 173
estate. *See also* estate planning
after death, person overseeing the, 134–135
auction, for getting rid of items, 129
farm, dividing, 50–52
heir as settler of, 133

joint, 30
settling, 17, 159–169
taxable, reducing, 63–65
estate planning. *See also* beneficiary designation; trusts; wills
creating comprehensive, 4–5
decision in naming heirs, 29–33
decisions of, 38–39
distributing legacy, 99–103
goals, 2, 110, 111
Medicaid trust and, 53, 56
overview of, 1–5
proactive, 107
process, 1
purpose of, 102
successful, vii
updating, naming heirs and, 30
using beneficiary designations, 67–68
estate planning attorney, consulting in naming heirs, 30
estates and protected individuals code (excerpt), 171–172
state taxes
defined, 173
strategies for, 33
executor
choosing, 105, 120, 134–135
defined, 173
naming, 41–42

F

fairness and equality, as strategy prior to death, 101
fair treatment, as legal right of beneficiaries, 93
families
conflict resolution, 79–80
dynamics, considering, 121–124
farm business, multi-generational, 50–52
helping, 3–4
irrevocable beneficiaries and, 9
loss and grief, 99
in naming heirs, 29, 30
protection of members, in partnership business, 49
family businesses, 47–52
business partnership, 48
farm, 50
keeping business after death, 51–52

180   **Beneficiary Guide for Everyone**

selling, 51
selling products, 51–52
using succession planning attorneys
for, 131
family cottage/(camp/cabin/vacation
property). *See* joint ownership,
problems solutions
federal Firearms License (FFL), 130
FFL. *See* Federal Firearms License
(FFL)
fiduciary, defined, 173
Fiduciary Act: Powers of the Law
to Control Wayward Trustees,
171–172
financial advisor, naming heirs and
consulting, 30
financial and practical concerns, loss,
grief, and, 100
financial goals
irrevocable beneficiaries and, 9
reassessing, 142
firearms, getting rid of, 130
five-year look-back period, irrevocable
Medicaid trusts and, 54, 57
flexibility, revocable beneficiaries and,
7–8
focusing on relationships, as strategy
prior to death, 101–102
Form 1040 income tax return, 163,
164
Form 1041S income tax return, 164
fraud, contesting a will and, 84
fraudulent Conveyance Act, 8
funeral arrangement, for armed forces
death, 159

G

gathering evidence, will and, 90
gifts, 63–65
consequences of gifting taxes,
64–65
loss of flexibility and, 65
Medicaid eligibility and estate
recovery, 65
reducing taxable estate, 63–65
glossary, 173–175
grantors/settlors
beneficiaries and, 13–17
death of, 10–11, 26, 37
revocable trusts and, 54
signing deed transferring title,
59–60

grief
as an individual process, 101
stages of, 99–100
study on, 99
guardian, 144, 145, 173
guide to manage and transfer digital
assets, 155–157
guilt and regret, loss, grief, and, 100

H

healthcare proxy documents, 32–33
heirlooms (family), getting rid of, 129
heirs
adding names to deeds, 64
asset management for, 2
credit cards payment and, 88
decisions on naming, 29–33
defined, 173
disabled, revocable trust and, 14
helping, 3–4
legitimate needs and wants of,
105–107
money management, revocable trust
and, 14
naming special needs heirs, 29
real estate with deed to, 124
as settler of estate, 133
state laws and determining, 13–14
"holographic will," 82, 83
How to Avoid Probate for Everyone
(Sharp), 59, 126
humankind, as beneficiary, 5

I

imprisonment, in partnership business,
49
incapacity, managing assets and
healthcare decisions, 52
income preservation, Medicaid trust
and, 53
incompetent persons, handling, 86–87,
89–90
individual circumstances
of beneficiaries, considering, 106
naming heirs and, 31
individual wishes, respecting deceased,
101
inflexibility, irrevocable beneficiaries
and, 9
information, as legal right of
beneficiaries, 93
in-ground burial, 137

Index

181

inheritance. *See also* heirs
  beneficiaries and consulting
    professionals in, 141–142
inherited property, disclaiming
  inheritance of, 79
inherited property with mortgage,
  guidance on, 72–73
  contacting the mortgage lender, 72
  contesting the will, 74
  disabled heirs and, 73–74
  leaving a child out of the will, 74
  minor children and, 73
  paying off mortgage, 73
  refinancing mortgage, 73
  reviewing mortgage terms, 72
  seeking professional advice, 73
  taking over mortgage under same
    conditions, 72
intangible assets, 1
intentions, communicating, 120–121
internal Revenue Service (IRS), in
  computing corporate valuation, 166
intestacy, laws of, 82–83
intestate, defined, 174
inventory, personal property and
  making, 44–45
investing, for the future, 142
investments and investment objectives,
  reviewing after death, 167–169
investment trustee, 25
irrevocable beneficiaries, 7
  advantages of, 8–9
  disadvantages of, 9
  scenario, 10
irrevocable Medicaid trusts, 54
irrevocable trust, revocable trust *vs.*,
  3, 10–11
issue, defined, 174

J

jewelry, getting rid of, 129
joint assets, 16, 26
joint co-trustees, 120
joint marital situation, in estate planning
joint ownership, problems solutions,
  35–36
joint tenancy, defined, 174
joint trusts, 120
joint with right of survivorship
  (JWROS), 62, 63
JWROS. *See* joint with right of
  survivorship (JWROS)

L

ladybird deed, 59–62, 124
  as planning tool, 59–60
  recording at the state office before
    grantors death, 60
  transfer on death deed, 61–62
laws. *See also* states laws
  on burial practices, 138
  of intestacy, 82–83
  local, naming heirs and, 32
  of Medicaid, 54
  on requirements and limitations of
    pet trusts, 152
lawyer consultation
  for family-owned businesses, 131
  for guidance and peace of mind, 71
  in proving a will, 90–91
  for will and trust, 71–72
legacy distribution, in heartfelt way,
  99–103
legal advices, as legal right of
  beneficiaries to seeking, 94
legal obligations, considering, 106
legal process
  estate planning and, 3
  proving a will and participation
    in, 91
legal requirements, settling trust-based
  estate and, 70–71
legal rights, of beneficiaries
  loosing or missing documents,
    96–97
  most common rights, 93–95
life insurance
  policy, beneficiary designation and,
    67
  proceeds, 1–2
life tenant, defined, 174
living trusts
  as alternative of adding children's
    names to deed, 65
  defined, 174
Living Trusts for Everyone (Sharp), 3
long-term care planning, Medicaid
  trusts and, 55–56
look-back period, five-year. irrevocable
  Medicaid trusts and, 54, 57

M

marriages, previous, naming heirs and
  asset from, 30
Mausoleum burial, 137

182   Beneficiary Guide for Everyone

mediation
  proving a will and, 91
  resolving disputes and, 32
Medicaid. *See also* Medicaid trusts
  benefits, 54
  eligibility and estate recovery, 65
  irrevocable Medicaid trusts, 54
  planning, ladybird deeds and, 61
  planning, special needs trusts and, 55
  qualification, irrevocable
    beneficiaries and, 9
  qualification and asset management,
    53–54
  revocable Medicaid trusts, 54
Medicaid trusts, 53–54
  irrevocable, 54
  legal considerations in, 55–57
  practical application of, 55–57
medical advances, as beneficiary, 5
Michigan statute, 171–172
military discharge papers, in settling
  estate, 159
military personnel, wills for, 92
minor children
  as beneficiary, 107–108, 115
  inheritance, revocable trust and, 14
  naming heirs and, 29–30
misuse potential, revocable
  beneficiaries and, 8–9
money, as beneficiary, 5
monitoring and oversight, trust
  protector and, 26
mortgage property inheritance. *See*
  inherited property with mortgage,
  guidance on

N
natural burial, 137
neutral executor appointment, naming
  heirs and, 31
notarization, of will, 82
nursing home transitioning, Medicaid
  trusts and, 56

O
On Death and Dying (Kübler-Ross),
  99
open and transparent communication,
  as strategies prior to death, 101, 102
oral wills and trusts, 86, 96
organizations, for getting rid of items,
  129

ownership. *See also* joint ownership
  of digital assets, transfer of, 156
  gift as permanent transfer of, 62
  IRA and changing, 67
  joint, 63–65
  property, ladybird deed ad retaining
    rights, 61
  property, transferring ladybird deed
    and, 61
  at time of death, 1

P
partnership business, 48
  employees' obligations in, 49
  protection of family members in, 49
  things to consider in, 49
  valuing buyout, 48
  valuing customer list, 48–49
pay on death (POD), 121–122, 174
peace of mind, attorney to provide, 71
per capita beneficiary, 118
percentages, beneficiaries and using,
  68
performance-based disbursements, as
  beneficiary condition, 117
personal circumstances, irrevocable
  beneficiaries and, 9
personal property, making inventory
  of, 44–45
personal representative
  appointing, 22–23, 134–135
  authority of, 20, 147
  changes to the trust and, 20
  defined, 174
  naming, 40–41
personal values, naming heirs and,
  30–32
per stripes beneficiary, 118
pet trusts
  about, 151
  legality of, 151
  pets as beneficiaries, 151–152
  points to include in forming,
    152–153
physical and emotional symptoms,
  loss, grief, and, 100
planning
  ahead, death and, 101
  creating, 119–124
  Medicaid, 56, 61
  post-death and pre death, 1
  stages of, 1–5

Index

183

succession, 47
updating, naming heirs and, 20
POD. *See* Pay on death (POD)
pooled trusts, 55
pour-over will, 120
power of attorney
  after death, 20
  agent and, 19, 20, 21
  creating, 19–23
  defined, 19
  time limit of, 20
powers of appointment, 2, 20
prepared legal service, documents
  preparation and, 71–72
primary adviser to settle estate
  checking estate taxes, 161, 163
  checking the outside assets, 161,
    162–163
  distributing personal effects, 161,
    166–167
  ensuring that assets are within trust,
    161, 162–163
  filing income tax returns, 161,
    163–164
  notifying life insurance companies,
    161, 162
  obtaining written valuation of
    assets, 161, 164–165
  reviewing allocation and
    distribution, 161, 167
  reviewing business agreements,
    161, 166
  reviewing credit cards, 161, 166
  reviewing the living trust
    document, 161, 162
  reviewing the size of estate, 161, 163
  settling estate and meeting with,
    161
  steps to settle an estate in living
    trust, 161–169
primary beneficiary, 117
"principal"
  agent and, 19
  allowing the power, 20
priorities, naming heirs and, 30–31
privacy
  as legal right of beneficiaries, 94
  revocable trust and, 14
probate, 144. *See also* probate
  avoidance; probate courts
  advantages of, 15
  case of, 125–126

costs of, 15, 20
defined, 174
filing for estate, 22–23
passing asset by gifting without, 63
purpose of, 81–82
revocable trust and, 14
supervised, 95
trust not required to go through, 15
probate avoidance, 2, 3
  adding names of heirs to deed for,
    64
  ladybird deed and, 59–60
  problem of probate judge and, 78
  situations of, 20–21
probate courts, 15, 21, 42
  authority on the trust issue, 42, 78
  heirs disagreement and, 45
  properly drafted estate plan and
    avoiding, 78
probate process, handling, 98
professional advice, naming heirs and
  consulting, 30, 141
professional trustee, 38, 108, 120
Promession burial, 138

Q

qualified domestic trust, defined,
  174–175

R

reading the will, 143–145
real estate
  decision on the inherited property,
    142
  gifting and, 63
  to heirs with deed, 124
removal and replacement of trustees,
  trust protector and, 26–27
resultant trustee, 25
revocable beneficiaries, 7, 118
  advantages of, 7–8
  disadvantages of, 8
  scenario, 10
revocable living trust, as beneficiary,
  122
revocable living trusts/revocable
  trusts
  benefits to deceased and long-term
    management, 14
  defined, 175
  vs. irrevocable trusts, 10–11
revocable Medicaid trusts, 54–55

184 Beneficiary Guide for Everyone

S

safe-deposit box, settling estate and locking up, 160
safeguarding beneficiary interests, trust protector and, 27
separate assets, revocable trust and, 14
Settling Estates for Everyone (Sharp), 17
"settling the estate," 159
  settlement process, 161–169
  upon death, 159–161
 700.1308, 171–172
simplicity, revocable beneficiaries and, 8
skill acquisition, as beneficiary condition, 117
small business, defined, 47
social Security, death and end of, 87–88
social withdrawal, loss, grief, and, 100
special burial, 138
special circumstances
  of beneficiaries, considering, 106
  naming heirs and, 32–33
special IRS Trust Identification Number, using, 164
special needs trusts, 53–57
specific beneficiary, 118
spendthrift provision, 124–126
spendthrifts, trustees for, 108–110
spousal rights, naming heirs and, 29
"springing" power, 18
state-level inheritance taxes, 64
state regulations. *See* states laws
states laws
  determining inheritance of children, 94–95
  ladybird deeds and, 60–61
  Medicaid programs and, 54
  relying on, 13
  rights to beneficiaries and, 94
  wills and, 2
stuff. *See* tangible personal property
succession planning, 47
successor trustee, 161
  on location of safe-deposit box and key, 160
  trust protector acting as, 27
supervised probate, 95, 97

T

tag sales, for getting rid of items, 129
tangible assets, 1, 3
tangible personal property, 127–132
taxable estate reduction, pros and cons, 63–65
tax benefits, irrevocable beneficiaries and, 8
taxes. *See also* estate taxes
  consequences of gift taxes, 64–65
  consideration, writing will and trust and, 71
  joint ownership and, 63–64
  Medicaid trusts and implication of, 55
  state-level inheritance, 64
tenants by the entireties, defined, 175
"tenants in common," 175. *See* also joint ownership
testamentary capacity, 89
  lack of, contesting a will and, 83–84
  writing your will and, 69
testate, defined, 175
testator
  defined, 175
  naming heirs and intent of, 31
testator's intent. considering wishes and, 106
timeline, proving a will and, 91
timeshares, selling, 131–132
TOD. *See* Transfer on death (TOD)
transfer-on-death deeds, as alternative of adding children's names to deed, 65
transfer on death (TOD), 122. *See also* Pay on death (POD)
treating self, portion of inheritance, 142
trust-based estate settlement, 123
trust beneficiary, 118
trust companies, 38, 120
trust directors, 25–27. *See also* trust protector
  defined, 25–26
  duties of, 25
  overseeing trustees, 25
trustees, 15
  agent for children of spendthrifts, 108–110
  choosing, 120
  defined, 175

Index

directed, 25
duties of, 25
joint co-trustees, 120
naming co-trustees, 37–38, 39–40
naming heirs and appointing, 31
professional, 38, 120
removal and replacement of, 26–27
responsibilities of, 16
selection, Medicaid and, 55
successor, trust protector acting
   as, 27
trusting, 37–42
trust modification, trust protector
   and, 26
trust protector
   appointment of, 26
   compensation of, 26
   power of, 25–26
   role and responsibilities of, 26
trusts. *See also* pet trusts
   advantage of naming as beneficiary,
      124
   beneficiary designation of, 113–126
   benefit of carefully prepared, 80
   challenging, 85–86
   corporation and, 15
   cottage, 36
   downside of, 16
   dying without, 13
   embezzlement of, 149–150
   for estate planning, 10–11, 15,99
   familiarity with and establishing, 4
   grantors and change of, 37
   irrevocable Medicaid trusts, 54
   joint, 120
   as legal entity, 15
   modification or amendment, 26
   oral, 86
   personal representative and changes
      to, 20
   person in charge of, 16
   pooled, 55
   vs. probatable will, using, 123–124
   problems of, 77–78
   protection against Medicaid
      recovery, 56
   reasons for creating, 77
   revocable Medicaid trusts, 54–55

special needs, 29, 53–57
updating documents, 52
writing your own, 68–75

U

undue influence, contesting a will and,
   83–84
unmarried persons, revocable trust
   and, 14

V

video taking, for interviews, 90

W

"what ifs" in estate planning, 2–3
will contests
   challenges without evidence, 85
   coercion or undue influence, 84
   contesting portions of will, 84–85
   filing to contest, 85
   fraud, 84
   grounds for objection, 86–90
   improper drafting or execution, 83
   lack of testamentary capacity, 83–84
   no-contest clause and, 85
   process of proving a will, 90–92
   reasons for invalid will, 83–90
wills. *See also* will contests
   as alternative of adding children's
      names to deed, 65
   beneficiary designation of, 113–126
   benefit of carefully prepared, 80
   changing, 43–44
   dying without, 13
   embezzlement of, 149–150
   familiarity with, 4
   filing with the court, 84
   holographic, 82, 83
   instruction, 147–150
   for military personnel, 92
   oral, 96
   probatable *vs.* trusts, 123–124
   reading ceremony, 143–145
   successor trustee and changes to, 20
   updating document, 52
   writing your own, 68–75
witnessing, of will, 82, 83, 92

Books from Allworth Press

Estate Planning for the Healthy, Wealthy Family
by Carla Garrity, Mitchell Baris, and Stanley Neeleman (6 × 9, 256 pages, ebook, $6.99)

Estate Planning (in Plain English)®
by Leonard D. DuBoff and Amanda Bryan (6 × 9, 336 pages, paperback, $19.99)

Feng Shui and Money (Second Edition)
by Eric Shaffert (6 × 9, 256 pages, paperback, $19.99)

How to Avoid Probate for Everyone
by Ronald Farrington Sharp (5½ × 8¼, 192 pages, paperback $14.99)

How to Plan and Settle Estates
by Edmund Fleming (6 × 9, 272 pages, paperback, $16.95)

Legal Forms for Everyone (Seventh Edition)
by Carl W. Battle and Andrea D. Small (8½ × 11, 328 pages, paperback, $26.99)

Legal Guide to Social Media (Second Edition)
by Kimberly A. Houser (6 × 9, 216 pages, paperback, $19.99)

Living Trusts for Everyone (Second Edition)
by Ronald Farrington Sharp (5½ × 8¼, 192 pages, paperback $16.99)

Love & Money
by Ann-Margaret Carrozza with foreword by Dr. Phil McGraw (6 × 9, 240 pages, paperback, $19.99)

The Money Mentor
by Tad Crawford (6 × 9, 272 pages, paperback, $24.95)

Protecting Your Assets from Probate and Long-Term Care
by Evan H. Farr (6 × 9, 208 pages, paperback, $14.99)

Settling Estates for Everyone
by Ronald Farrington Sharp (5½ × 8¼, 216 pages, paperback, $16.99)

The Secret Life of Money
by Tad Crawford (6 × 9, 312 pages, paperback, $19.99)

To see our complete catalog or to order online, please visit *www.allworth.com*.